The Secret Garden
IN CROSS STITCH

Rosaceae

Canary Bird

Golden Wings

'Dainty Bess'

Compassion

Harriny

Sea Pearl

The Secret Garden
IN CROSS STITCH

THEA GOUVERNEUR

WITH

HEATHER DEWHURST

MEREHURST

I dedicate this book to my parents, for a happy childhood and for supporting my art education during the hard times after the war. My dearest mother was always my biggest fan; both warm and hospitable, she taught me to respect other people. My father's perseverance and optimism have given me encouragement throughout.

First published in 1999
by Merehurst Ltd, Ferry House, 51–57 Lacy Road, Putney, London SW15 1PR

Designs copyright © Thea Gouverneur 1999

Text, photographs and illustrations copyright © Merehurst Ltd 1999 (except those listed below)

Thea Gouverneur has asserted her right under the Copyright, Designs and Patents Act, 1988

ISBN 1 85391 762 1

A catalogue record of this book is available from the British Library.

Text by Thea Gouverneur with Heather Dewhurst
Senior Commissioning Editor: Karen Hemingway
Project Editor: Rowena Curtis
Design: Maggie Aldred and Sarah Stanley
Photography: Michelle Garrett
Illustrations: King & King Design Associates
Publishing Manager: Fia Fornari
Production Manager: Lucy Byrne
CEO & Publisher: Anne Wilson
International Sales Director: Kevin Lagden
Marketing & Sales Director: Kathryn Harvey

Colour separation by Colourscan, Singapore; printed in Singapore by CS Graphics

All photographs by Michelle Garrett, © Merehurst Ltd, except the following:
THE GARDEN PICTURE LIBRARY: Tommy Candler, p115; Brian Carter, pp26L, 29;
Christi Carter, p74; Geoff Dann, p110L; John Glover, pp38L, 56L, 77, 78L;
Lamontagne, p84L; Mayer/Le Scanff, pp123, 125; Clive Nichols, p75; Laslo Puskas, p88L;
Howard Rice, p126; Gary Rogers, p96L; Christel Rosenfeld, p134L; Michel Viard, p130L;
MEREHURST LTD: pp7, 10L, 11, 98L, 120; MURDOCH BOOKS: pp12L, 97; Lorna Rose,
© MURDOCH BOOKS: pp6, 8, 9, 18R, 22 above, 25, 34, 36L, 37, 42L, 46, 48L, 54, 55,
57, 58, 66, 68L, 76R, 80, 82, 83, 94, 95, 104L, 106, 116L, 124R; Graham L. Strong: pp35, 53.

Contents

Inspirations

I think I was born with a passion for flowers. My father was a bulb grower and exporter, as was my mother's father in a neighbouring village; my father and my mother's brother first met on a boat bound for America where they were going to sell flowers. Ever since I can remember, flowers have been part of my life. When I began to draw, and later to stitch, it seemed natural to choose flowers as my inspiration.

I GREW UP in the village of Sassenheim in The Netherlands, surrounded by bulb fields. When I looked out of my bedroom window in spring and summer I could see row upon row of flowers, stretching as far as the eye could see. My brothers, sisters and I would help in the bulb fields during the spring and summer holidays, harvesting the flowers in readiness for export to the UK, Germany and the USA. First it was the daffodils, tulips and hyacinths, later the irises, dahlias and gladioli. We would cut the flowers by hand using a blade, working up and down the rows, and piling the cut flowers in one corner of the field. It was backbreaking work, but we enjoyed it.

As my father was always busy in the fields, it was my job to do the gardening at home, but it was a chore that I loved. I had green fingers and enjoyed planting and pruning as well as weeding. My favourite flowers were the sweet peas which would scramble up one wall of the house, their fragile scented petals quivering in the slightest breeze. I began to draw and sketch in the garden at home, which is when I developed an eye for detail. I wanted to make my drawings of flowers look exactly like they do in real life.

My other passion was sewing, a skill I inherited from my mother. She used to give me offcuts of fabric and I would make clothes for our dolls. It was my aunt who first encouraged me to try embroidery. I used to stay with her each summer, and she was always embroidering exquisite panels, cushions and kneelers which were sold for the church. I was fascinated by the way her needle would flash in and out of the fabric, stitching tiny stitches with lustrous coloured threads. She showed me how to draw a pattern on fabric with a pencil, then embroider over it with twisted chain stitches, French knots and satin stitches. I took to embroidery quickly, and spent much of my spare time after that making pictures with coloured threads.

My love of designing led me to the Royal Academy of Art in The Hague, where I completed a teaching course in drawing and fashion design. It was while I was teaching that I began to design my

own cross stitch flower designs. Some years later I made charts from these initial designs and a friend suggested I should sell them, so I approached a department store in Amsterdam who immediately offered to sell them for me. I set up in business designing and selling kits, which is what I have been doing for the past three decades, with great enjoyment.

Although I now design on a computer, the way I approach each design is still the same. I study the flowers themselves, either in the garden, in the countryside, or I take photographs and compose a picture from several different ones.

People sometimes ask me where I get the inspiration for my designs, a question which never fails to surprise me. I always answer: look out of your window and you will see inspiration everywhere – in gardens, in hedgerows, in fields, woods and hills. There are so many beautiful flowers, plants, bushes and trees growing, that there is not enough time to stitch them all. I know that I will never run out of ideas; it is much more likely that I will run out of time first! Before I do, however, I am delighted that I have been able to include some of my flower designs in this book. They are all very detailed as I like

to use lots of different colour threads. Some cross stitchers might find this fiddly, but I think it is worth it as the end results are realistic and true to nature. Although the designs might take you longer to complete, I hope you have great pleasure stitching them and, as you gaze on the finished pieces, I hope they will remind you of the wonderful glory of nature.

Thea Gouverneur, Sassenheim

Bulb fields

Bulb flowers have long been revered for their beauty. In Ancient Greece the lily was regarded as a symbol of purity and paintings of lilies decorated the walls of Cretan palaces. The great civilizations of Greece, Egypt, India and China grew bulb flowers, including lilies, crocuses, cyclamen, narcissi, gladioli and irises, for their highly decorative qualities.

Bulb fields projects

TULIP DISPLAY CUSHION

BULB FLOWER PANELS

GLADIOLI PANELS

ALTHOUGH MY native country, The Netherlands, has long been regarded as the leading bulb nation, bulb flowers were not introduced to the western world until the 16th century. Bulbs first entered Europe via the Ottoman Empire, where they were sold in the flower shops of Constantinople.

Tulips, in particular, caught the imagination of the West and a period of 'tulip mania' gripped the Dutch flower market in the 17th century. Prices of rare bulbs rocketed, and some desperate buyers even sold their possessions in order to buy the precious bulbs. The most sought-after tulips were those with feathered, flamed or streaked blooms. It soon reached the stage when demand began to exceed supply and promissory notes were sold from one investor to another. The market eventually crashed when, in 1647, the Dutch government declared that all such promissory notes had to be honoured with bulbs.

Bulb flowers only began to become more accessible for the general public in the 19th century, when prices fell. However, their popularity waned during this period as well, and bulbs began to be regarded as flowers fit only for 'shopkeepers and workers'. Luckily this class distinction has now been swept away and bulbs can be enjoyed by everyone. Bright bulb flowers are a common sight in gardens and parks in spring. They are also readily available from florists.

One of the reasons that bulb flowers are grown successfully in The Netherlands is the type of soil. The soil along the Dutch coast contains a high percentage of sand and salt, which has proved to be the ideal base for bulbs to grow in. The soil is kept well drained so the bulbs do not become waterlogged, and the salt helps to provide the nutrients the bulbs need. It is also possible that through centuries of practice the Dutch have the necessary business acumen to succeed in growing bulbs for export, although as the daughter of a bulb grower I am probably biased!

I consider myself lucky to have grown up among the bulb fields, and I know that my life has been immeasurably enriched by these flowers. My most vivid childhood memory is of the wonderful depth and variety of the colours. From spring to summer, the bulb fields were alive with colour – from the fresh yellow and white narcissi to pink and deep purple hyacinths, blushing pink and scarlet tulips, bright red dahlias and flame-coloured gladioli. It is hardly a surprise that bulb flowers are among my favourite flowers, both to grow in the garden and to pick to bring into the house.

Miniature varieties of each bulb are also grown in the fields. These delicate flowers are becoming more and more popular nowadays and look especially pretty growing in small gardens and rockeries. In my own garden I grow a variety of bulb flowers, including several types of tulip, yellow and purple crocus, blue hyacinths and of course narcissi, which are my favourite among all bulb flowers. Not only do they look beautiful, but after the long grey days of winter they herald the new season of spring with such style and colour that it is impossible not to be lifted by the sight of them.

In addition to their glorious colours, I love bulb flowers for their perfumes. I like to grow the bunch-flowered narcissi 'Paperwhite', with their small, dainty flower heads, indoors in pots. They have a very strong perfume which reminds me of home, as my father always had them in the house while I was growing up.

Many types of bulb flower are perfect for cutting and bringing indoors for use in flower arrangements. Most are best picked before they are fully open. Tulips, in particular, are ideal. Their stems bend and twist into marvellous shapes after they have been in water for a few days. Narcissi also keep well indoors as long as the water is changed regularly. Even dainty hyacinths and snowdrops can look pretty as a simple table centre arrangement, just placed in a jam jar filled with water.

Although bulb flowers, in their infinite variety of bold shapes and vibrant colours, provide endless inspiration for my designs, I have limited the number of bulb designs to one chapter in this book. Hopefully this will be just enough to see you through the depths of winter until the spring bulbs start flowering again. Try experimenting by working some of these designs on coloured linen – the single 'Tulip' looks particularly striking when stitched on black linen. Alternatively, the 'Gladioli' project offers a choice of colourways, and can be embroidered in red or in yellow.

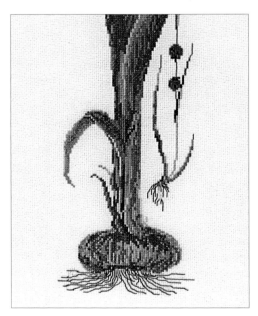

Tulip display

THIS TULIP design is one of my favourites. The sight of a field of tulips in bloom reminds me of when I was young. In the spring, when all the bulb fields were flowering, we used to cut lots of flowers for the house. I have always especially liked the yellow tulips with dark brown stamens. Try putting your nose into one of these flowers, closing your eyes and breathing in the delicious sweet scent.

The tulip has a fascinating history. Originating from the East, tulips were introduced into the West in the 16th century and there are now hundreds of varieties grown. The tulip's distinctive shape is reflected in its name, which comes from the Turkish word *tulband*, meaning turban. The ideal tulip should be shaped like an almond and the leaves should look as thin and tapering as daggers.

Tulip display cushion

The finished design measures
29 x 29cm (11½ x 11½in)

YOU WILL NEED

*28-count blue or white linen,
approx. 34 x 34cm (13¾ x 13¾in)
Stranded embroidery thread
as given in the key
No. 24 tapestry needle
Yellow 'desert sand' linen
Coffee-coloured linen
Cream calico
Needles, pins and thread
3 buttons*

THE EMBROIDERY

1 Prepare the piece of linen in your chosen colour, as outlined on pages 138–140. Find the centre of the fabric and carefully mark the central vertical and horizontal lines with basting stitches.

2 Find the centre of the chart and mark it for your reference. With one strand of embroidery thread in the needle, begin stitching the design from this point, working each cross stitch over two threads of the fabric, and ensuring that all the upper threads of the stitch go in the same direction. Follow the chart to complete the

cross stitching; each square of the chart
represents one stitch.

FINISHING

1 Remove the finished embroidery from
the hoop or frame and hand wash it in
warm water. Then lay it face down on a
towel and press with a hot iron until dry.

2 Turn under the ends of the embroidery
and press with a hot iron. Place the
embroidery face upwards on a piece of
sand-coloured linen measuring 42 x 41cm
(16$^{1/2}$ x 16in), ensuring that it is centred.
Pin and topstitch around the edges, about
2mm ($^{1/16}$in) from the edge.

3 Turn under the edges of the sand-
coloured linen by about 1cm ($^{1/2}$in) and
press. Centre this on a piece of coffee-
coloured linen measuring 48 x 48cm (19 x
19in). Pin and topstitch around the edges,
about 2mm ($^{1/16}$in) from the edge.

4 Cut two pieces of cream calico, one
measuring 48 x 31.5cm (19 x 12$^{3/4}$in) and
another measuring 48 x 30cm (19 x 12in).
Take the first piece and turn under one of
its shorter ends by 5cm (2in). Pin and stitch
4cm (1$^{1/2}$in) from the edge, then press.
Take the second piece of calico and turn
under one of its shorter ends by 1.5cm
($^{5/8}$in), stitch and press.

5 Stitch up the cushion cover, following
the instructions on pages 138–141, then
sew the buttons on to the back flap. Insert
a cushion pad to complete. For a project
of this size use a cushion pad measuring
45 x 45cm (18 x 18in).

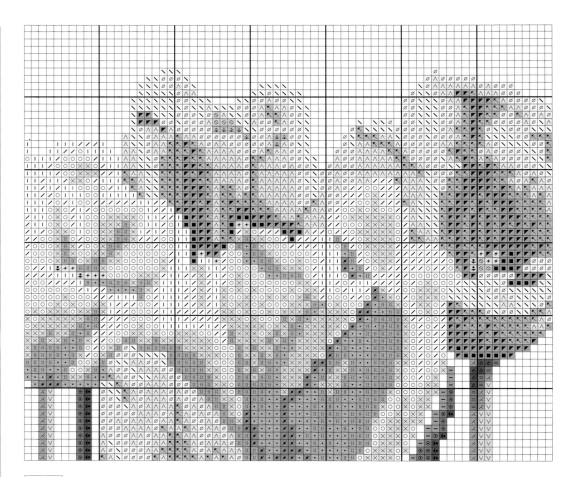

A

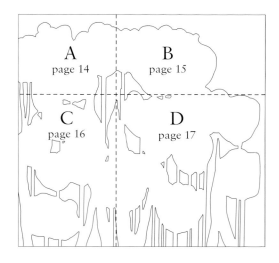

A page 14 B page 15
C page 16 D page 17

*The chart for the 'Tulip display'
cushion has been split over four pages.
Refer to this diagram to check the
relevant page on which each section
of the chart falls.*

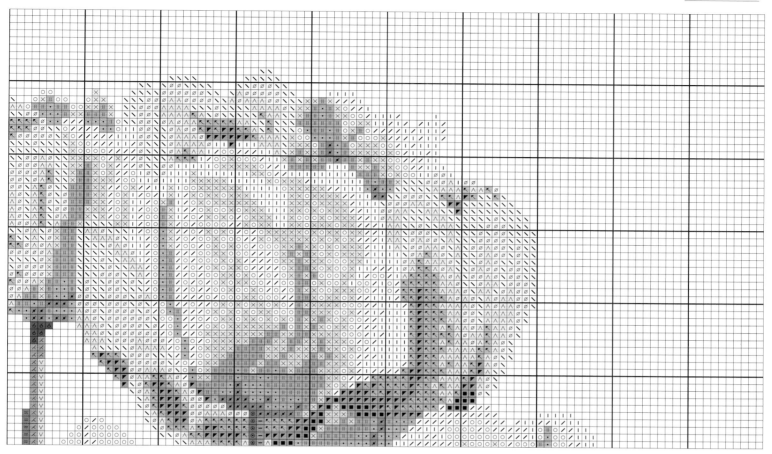

B

TULIP DISPLAY *key*

	DMC	ANCHOR
╱╱	746	275
○○	822	390
××	644	391
‖‖	642	392
··	640	393
◢◢	3790	904
╲╲	745	300
∅∅	677	361
∧∧	676	891
��	729	890
◤◤	680	901
■■	3829	901
△△	368	214
--	320	215
◉◉	367	216
◖◖	319	1044
◥◥	890	218
∨∨	3348	264
⋉⋉	3347	266
==	3346	267
66	3345	268
◤◤	895	1044
↯↯	725	305
♦♦	3820	306
‖‖	blanc	2
◎◎	834	874
▲▲	833	874
◥◥	832	907
✳✳	3371	382
⫼⫼	898	380
HH	989	242
MM	987	244
<<	986	246

16

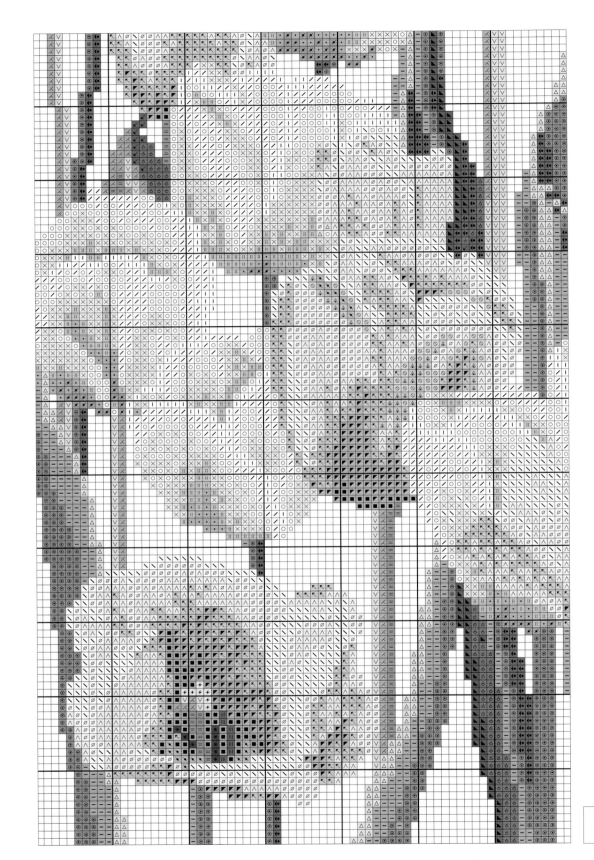

C

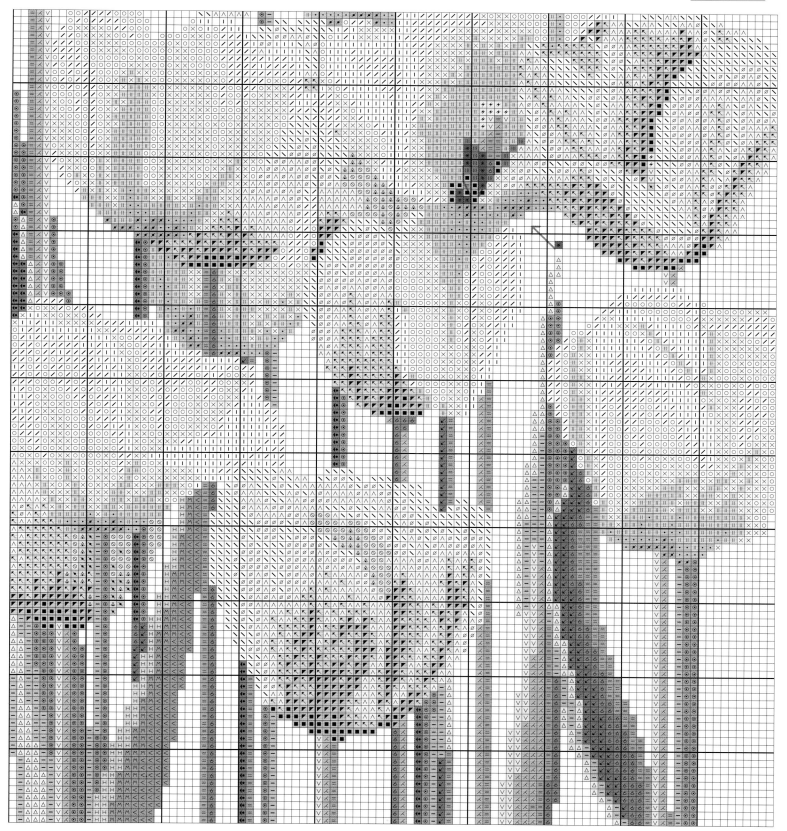

D

Bulb flowers

THESE DECORATIVE panels feature two of the most popular spring bulb flowers – the tulip and the daffodil. The red-and-cream petalled tulip is one of the lily-flowered tulips, an elegant variety with a distinctive shape. You can really appreciate the colour markings when the petals start to droop after the flowers have been in a vase of water for a few days.

Daffodils to me are the epitome of spring. Their cheerful yellow trumpets seem to herald the onset of sunshine after a long, dark winter. The yellow trumper daffodil, the 'Burgemeester Gouverneur', is special for me because it was named after my grandfather who was mayor (*burgemeester*) of one of the villages in the bulbflower region of Sassenheim for 20 years.

Bulb flower panels

Each finished panel measures
18 x 23cm (7 x 9in)

YOU WILL NEED

Three pieces of 36-count white linen,
approx. 29 x 25.5cm (11¹/₂ x 10in)
Stranded embroidery thread
as given in the key
No. 24 tapestry needle
Strong board or card
Strong thread for lacing
Mount and frame of your choice

THE EMBROIDERY

1 Cut out the fabric, bearing in mind the amount you would like to remain visible between the stitched design and the frame. The amount suggested above will result in approximately 7.5cm (3in) of unstitched fabric all around the design.

2 Prepare the piece of fabric as outlined on pages 138–140. Find the centre of the fabric and mark central vertical and horizontal lines with basting stitches.

3 Having chosen one of the three charts, find the centre of the chart and mark it for

your reference. Working with one strand of embroidery thread in the needle, begin stitching your preferred design from this central point. Work each cross stitch over two threads of the fabric, ensuring that the upper threads of each stitch go in the same direction.

4 Follow your chosen chart to complete the cross stitching; each square of the chart represents one stitch.

5 Complete the back stitch details as indicated on the chart, using one strand of embroidery thread in the needle. Refer to the key throughout for the colours of thread to be used.

FINISHING

1 When the stitching is complete, remove the finished embroidery from the hoop or frame and hand wash it carefully in warm water. Then lay the embroidery face down on a towel and press it gently with a hot iron until it is dry.

2 Choose a mount and frame for the embroidery that will co-ordinate with the colours in the design and with your home furnishings. Picking a colour that only features slightly in the stitching will serve to highlight it in the picture. If you have chosen to complete all three of the bulb flower charts in this project you may want to purchase three similar frames, as used in the photograph above. Then you can display them as a set.

3 Cut a piece of board or card to fit the frame and mount the piece of embroidery as explained on page 141. To finish, set the mount in the frame.

	DMC	ANCHOR
	3363	262
	3362	263
	762	234
	415	398
	318	235
	3716	25
	834	874
	676	891
	934	862
	3364	261
	3047	852
	3046	887
	760	1022
	3712	1023
	3045	888
	3328	1024
	347	1025
	761	1021
	640	393
	642	392
	blanc	2
	746	275
	822	390
	644	391

TULIP *key*

	DMC	ANCHOR
	369	1043
	966	240
	353	8
	352	9
	351	10
	350	11
	817	13
	819	271
	963	23
	833	874
	869	375
	3348	264

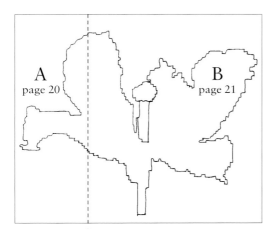

A
page 20

B
page 21

The chart for the 'Tulip' panel
has been split over two pages.
Refer to this diagram to see
how the chart fits together.

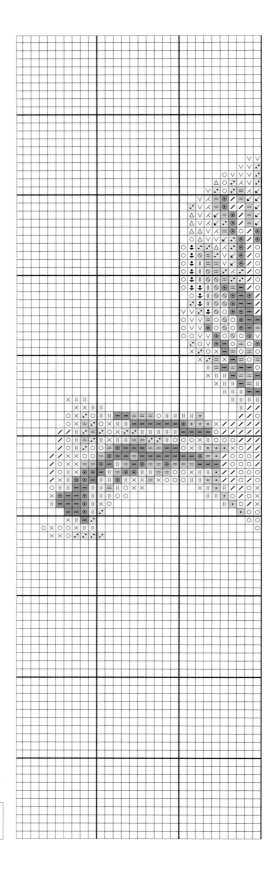

A

B

DAFFODIL *key*

	DMC	ANCHOR
∕ ∕	369	1043
○ ○	368	214
✕ ✕	320	215
‖ ‖	367	216
• •	319	1044
◤ ◤	890	218
＼ ＼	3823	386
∅ ∅	745	300
∧ ∧	744	301
◢ ◢	743	302
↖ ↖	725	305
△ △	677	361
⊙ ⊙	3822	295
＝ ＝	3820	306
◄ ◄	729	890
◣ ◣	3829	901
∨ ∨	472	253
✕ ✕	471	265
■ ■	3371	382
‑ ‑	822	390
✕ ✕	644	391
✦ ✦	642	392
6 6	640	393
↯ ↯	3790	904
❙ ❙	938	381
⊘ ⊘	898	380
▲ ▲	831	277

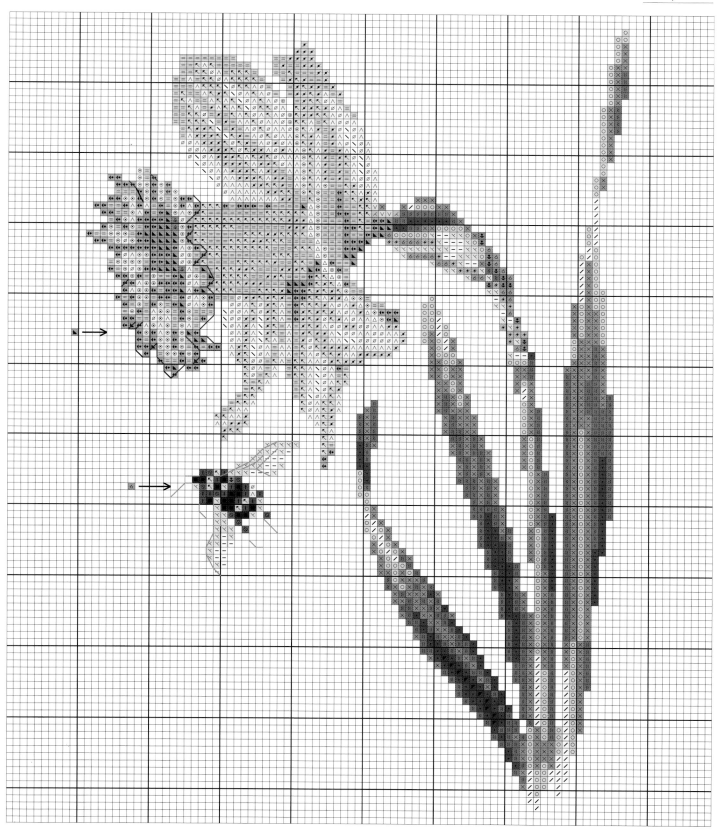

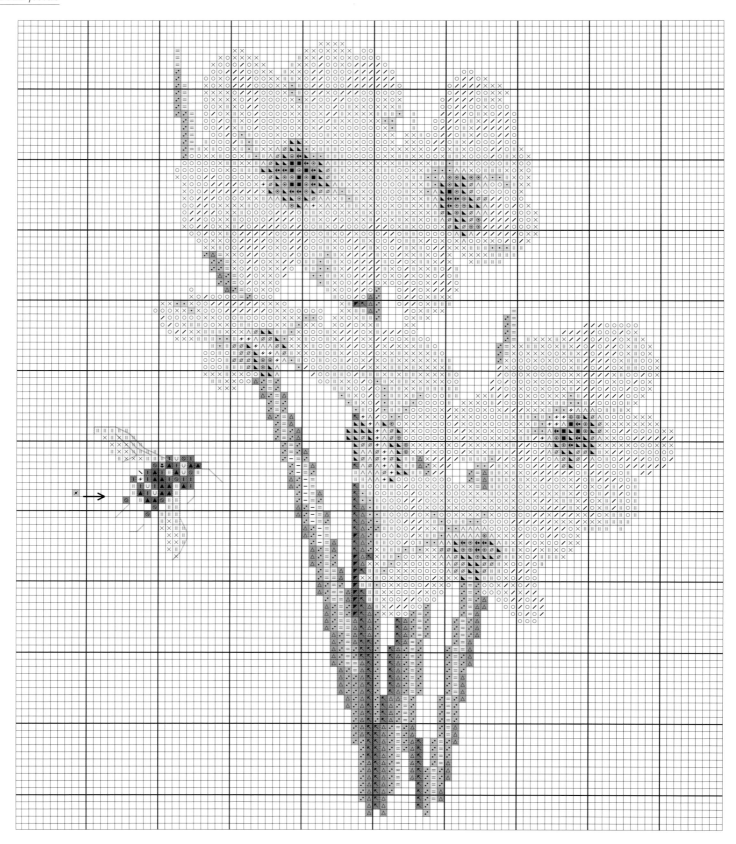

NARCISSUS *key*

	DMC	ANCHOR		DMC	ANCHOR
∕∕ ∕∕	blanc	2	↖↖ ↖↖	319	1044
○○ ○○	746	275	△△ △△	367	216
×× ××	822	390	∴∴	320	215
‖‖ ‖‖	644	391	== ==	368	214
∵∵	642	392	−− −−	369	1043
◢◢	640	393	⊙⊙ ⊙⊙	721	324
╲╲	745	300	◀◀ ◀◀	900	333
⚡⚡ ⚡⚡	744	301	■■ ■■	919	340
∧∧ ∧∧	743	302	∪∪ ∪∪	725	305
∅∅ ∅∅	742	303	▲▲ ▲▲	3371	382
◣◣	740	316	✦✦	3790	904
◤◤	890	218	⏐⏐ ⏐⏐	938	381
			⊘⊘ ⊘⊘	898	380

Gladioli

STATELY, DISTINGUISHED looking flowers, the tall spikes of magnificent trumpet-shaped gladioli are a familiar sight in summer flowerbeds. Their long tapering leaves give the flower its name; gladiolus actually comes from the Latin word *gladius*, meaning sword. Originating in Africa, gladioli were depicted in wall paintings in Pompeii, and were only introduced into the north of Europe in the 17th century. Now there are many varieties available, in every colour of the rainbow.

The two panels both follow the same chart, but are stitched in different colours. You could embroider the gladioli in any colour you choose, using light and dark shades accordingly. The only other difference is the detail added to the design: a buttercup and dragonfly with the yellow, flowering grass and ladybirds with the red.

Gladioli panels

Each finished design measures
12 x 81cm (4³/4 x 32in)

YOU WILL NEED

*18-count white Aida fabric,
approx. 26.5 x 96.5cm (10¹/2 x 38in)
Stranded embroidery thread
as given in the key
No. 24 tapestry needle
Strong board or card
Strong thread for lacing
Mount and frame
of your choice*

THE EMBROIDERY

1 Cut out the fabric, bearing in mind the amount of unstitched material that you would like to remain visible between the stitched design and the frame. The size of fabric suggested for this project will result in approximately 7.5cm (3in) of unstitched material all around the design.

2 Prepare the piece of Aida fabric for stitching as outlined on pages 138–140. Find the centre of the fabric and mark the central vertical and horizontal lines with basting stitches. Then find and mark the centre of the chart for your reference.

3 With one strand of embroidery thread in your needle, begin stitching the design from the central point, working each cross stitch over two strands of the Aida fabric. Ensure that all the upper threads of each stitch go in the same direction.

4 Follow the chart on the following pages to complete the stitching; each square of the chart represents one stitch.

5 Finally, complete the back stitch details, using one strand of embroidery thread in the needle and referring to the key for colours of thread to be used.

FINISHING

1 When the embroidery is complete, remove the finished piece from the hoop or frame and hand wash it carefully in warm water. Then lay the embroidery face down on a towel and press it with a hot iron until it is dry.

2 Choose a mount and frame that will co-ordinate with the colours in the design. Cut a piece of board or card to fit and mount the embroidery as explained on page 141. Set the mount in the frame.

yellow GLADIOLI *key*

	DMC	ANCHOR		DMC	ANCHOR
	369	1043		869	375
	368	214		471	265
	320	215		3364	261
	367	216		3781	1050
	319	1044		3031	905
	890	218		778	968
	814*	45*		3047	852
	746*	275*		3045	888
	3348	264		840	1084
	3820*	306*		738	361
	680*	901*		783	307
	677*	361*		731	281
	3822*	295*		991	1076
	3821*	305*		444	291
	321*	47*		445	288
	498*	1005*		993	1070
	815*	44*		433	358
	772	259		469	267
	3371	382		745	300
	831*	277*		741	304
	902*	897*		733	280
	316	1017		436	363
	3726	1018		935	861
	315	1019		898	380
	3802	896		955	206
	3347	266		954	203
	612	832		3013	853
	729	890		3829	901
	611	898		830	889
	310	403		414*	235*
	3052	844			

Follow this key when stitching the 'Gladioli' design in yellow. When stitching the design in red interchange all the colours marked * with those in the key on page 29.

red GLADIOLI *key*

	DMC	ANCHOR
⌀ ⌀ / ⌀ ⌀	744	301
∧ ∧ / ∧ ∧	352	9
◼	817	13
↖ ↖ / ↖ ↖	815	44
△ △ / △ △	351	10
∴ ∴	350	11
= = / = =	349	13
⊙ ⊙ / ⊙ ⊙	745	300
– – / – –	677	361
∨ ∨ / ∨ ∨	676	891
◼ ◼	814	45
× × / × ×	3340	329
◢ ◣	606	334

To stitch the 'Gladioli' design in red, follow the
key above, interchanging all the colours marked
* with the colours in this key.

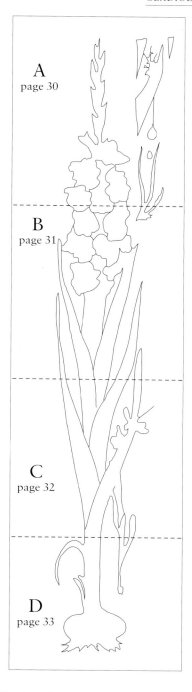

The chart for the 'Gladioli' panel has
been split over four pages. Refer to this
diagram to check the relevant page
on which each section of the chart falls.
Stitch the buttercup detail with the
yellow Gladioli and the meadowgrass
detail with the red Gladioli.

A

B

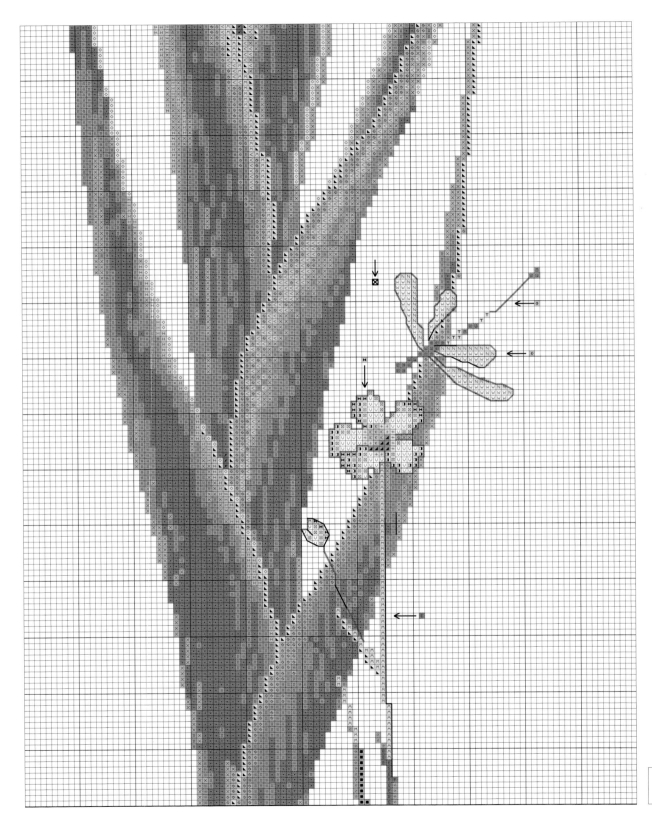

C

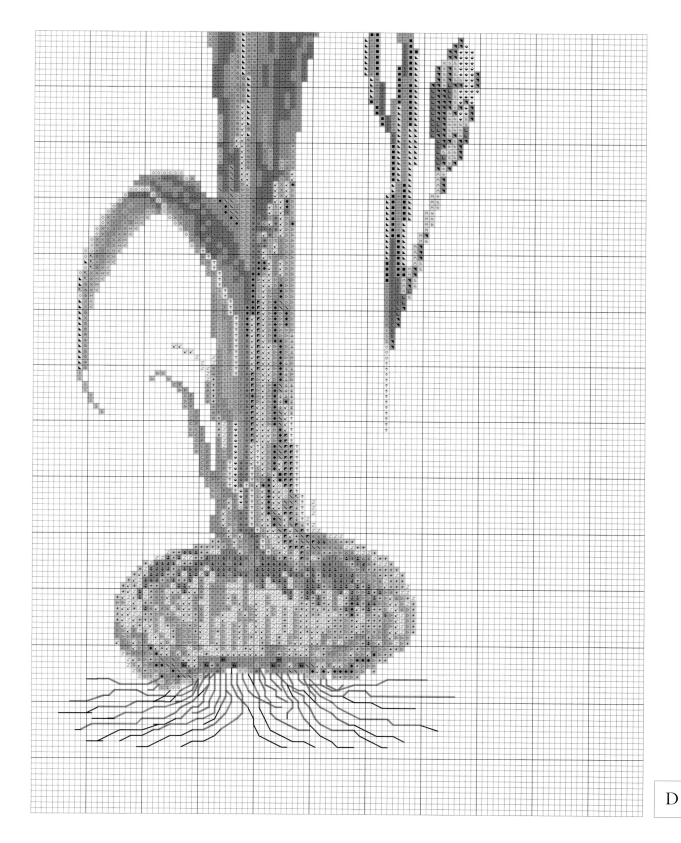

D

The joys of spring

Spring is always a wonderful time of year – a fascinating time of change and rejuvenation. Young plants are pushing their way out of the dark, cold earth, new pale green leaves are unfurling from sticky buds on the trees and, wherever you look, colourful flowers start to open, releasing the fresh scents, colours and sights of the new season.

The joys of spring
projects

FRITILLARIA PANEL

PEAR BLOSSOM LINEN

CROCUS PANEL

SNOWDROPS ARE among the first flowers to show their heads among the cold brown stems and dark earth in the garden and in between the tangled brambles in hedgerows. They are hailed as the messengers of spring, and are known to have been in existence for 2000 years. Their delicate nodding heads seem most unlikely to survive the end of winter winds and frost, yet surprisingly they do. Crocuses quickly follow in their wake, bringing with them carpets of brighter colour – golden yellow and shiny purple. The large funnel-shaped flowers appear before the long narrow leaves and open wide in the warm spring sun.

The beautiful fritillary is another flower that appears in spring. The majestic 'Crown Imperial' (*Fritillaria imperialis*) is one of the oldest garden plants and is also known as the Easter lily. The smaller 'Snake's head' fritillary (*Fritillaria meleagris*) can be a magical sight when found growing in damp spring meadows.

Gardens, too, seem to come alive at this time of year with the bright yellow and white trumpets of daffodils and narcissi and the clusters of yellow flowers along the bare branches of forsythia. Other bushes and shrubs start to thicken out with new leaves and shoots, blossom appears as if overnight on fruit trees, scarlet, orange and yellow tulips appear in mid-spring, and the dead, brown look of winter is suddenly replaced with an array of colour and abundance.

Springtime holds a number of special memories for me. When I was growing up in Sassenheim not only did we have the beauty of the surrounding bulb fields to enjoy in spring, we also had an annual flower festival and mosaic competition. During the festival week everyone made their gardens as pretty and decorative as possible. Initially, the festivals focused just on the spring hyacinth. The resulting scent from the gathered hyacinths was amazing.

The competition involved making a mosaic in your garden with blue and white hyacinth flowers. These mosaics developed into carpets of individual hyacinth florets, each only about 3cm (1¼in) high, which were laid out in a design that lasted for a week or so. I made one of my first hyacinth designs with a friend when we were both about eight years old. The mosaic depicted one of Disney's seven dwarves and I like to think that it was rather successful!

Making a mosaic picture is rather like charting a cross stitch design. You have to consider the various blocks of colour and the shading and highlights. It is necessary to keep standing back from your design to view it as a whole in order to see whether it works. This is something I still do today with each new cross stitch design I work on. The flower festivals still take place in the Sassenheim region today, although the flowers are now pinned into polystyrene rather than stuck into the garden, so that the designs are transportable.

Another memory I have of spring is of Easter. My sisters, brothers and I all believed in the Easter hare, and the story of how it would hide presents of chocolate eggs for all the children on Easter Day. Of course it was my parents, and not the Easter hare, who used to hide the eggs between the tulips,

daffodils and hyacinths in the garden. On Easter morning, my sisters, brothers and I would have to hunt for them.

Although I have given up hunting for chocolate eggs, I always get a feeling of optimism in the spring. With a renewed energy, I feel ready to tackle anything. This is the time for spring cleaning the home, sorting out cupboards, throwing out all sorts of clutter and for clearing the winter debris in the garden. Spring does bring a lifting of the spirits, and it makes me feel immeasurably happier knowing the grey days of winter are coming to an end. The weather is warmer, the days are lighter and longer and the cold pallor of winter is replaced by a warm pink blush.

The cross stitch designs included in this chapter were designed with this springtime optimism in mind. Featuring some of the lovely flowers you can see in spring, they will give you a taste of warmer days of summer yet to come.

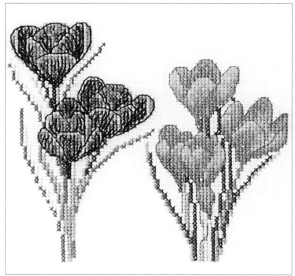

Fritillaria

T HE DIFFERENT flowers in the Fritillary family are similar in shape, with their bell-like blooms hanging gracefully from slender stems, suggesting shyness and delicacy. I have always delighted in these springtime flowers, as they provide a welcome sprinkling of colour in the garden and a promise of sunny days ahead.

The *Fritillaria imperialis* is also known as 'Crown Imperial', because it towers over other flowers in the garden. One story relates how when Jesus Christ was walking to Calvary, he passed a fritillary which refused to bend its head; ever since the bulbs have had an offensive smell and the fritillary head hangs permanently low. A smaller relation is the *Fritillaria meleagris*, or 'Snake's head', which is a delicate little flower. In some areas this flower grows wild, but it is a jewel in my garden.

Fritillaria panel

The finished design measures
17.5 x 26.5cm (7 x 10½in)

YOU WILL NEED

36-count white linen,
approx. 33 x 42cm (13¼ x 16½in)
Stranded embroidery thread
as given in the key
No. 24 tapestry needle
Strong board or card
Strong thread for lacing
Mount and frame of your choice

THE EMBROIDERY

1 Cut out the linen. The size of fabric suggested for this project will result in about 7.5cm (3in) of unstitched fabric around the cross stitch design.

2 Prepare the linen as outlined on pages 138–140. Find the centre of the fabric and carefully mark the central vertical and horizontal lines with basting stitches.

3 Find the centre of the 'Fritillaria' cross stitch chart and mark it for your reference. With one strand of embroidery thread in the needle, begin stitching the design from

Fritillaria meleagris

Fritillaria imperialis

this point, working each cross stitch over two threads of the fabric and ensuring that the upper threads of each stitch follow the same direction.

4 Follow the 'Fritillaria' chart to complete the cross stitching; each square of the chart represents one stitch.

5 Complete the back stitch details using one strand of embroidery thread in the needle, and referring to the key for the colours of thread to be used.

FINISHING

1 Remove the finished embroidery from the hoop or frame and hand wash it in warm water. Then lay it face down on a towel and press with a hot iron until dry.

2 Choose a mount and frame to suit the colours in the design. Cut a piece of board or card to fit the frame and mount the embroidery as explained on page 141. Set the mount in the frame.

Fritillaria

meleagris

A

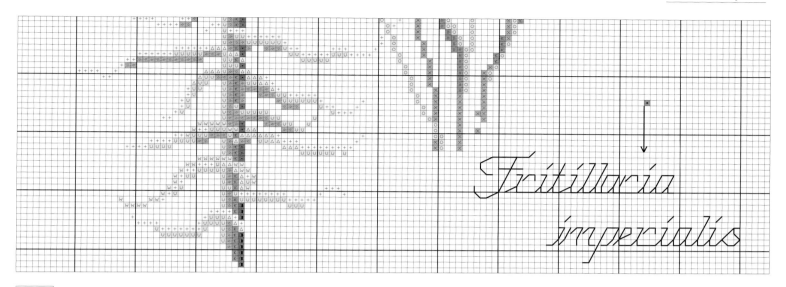

B

FRITILLARIA PANEL *key*

	DMC	ANCHOR		DMC	ANCHOR		DMC	ANCHOR
⁄⁄	369	1043		3347	266	◆◆	900	333
○○	368	214	KK	3346	267	△△	353	8
××	320	215	◻◻	3345	268	⋈⋈	352	9
‖‖	367	216	◤◤	895	1044	◥◥	3799	236
⠐⠐	319	1044	WW	613	831	▲▲	919	340
⠒⠒	890	218	33	blanc	2	ZZ	524	858
＼＼	746	275	⊡⊡	742	303	⌄⌄	316	1017
∅∅	822	390	⊖⊖	783	307	⬆⬆	3726	1018
∧∧	644	391	●●	780	309			
⊙⊙	642	392	>>	778	968			
△△	472	253	••	3802	1019			
∴	471	265	⊕⊕	902	897			
══	470	266	✦✦	3740	872			
──	469	267	⦙⦙	3822	295			
◂◂	936	846	↓↓	3047	852			
◥◥	935	861	◐◐	3046	887			
◤◤	934	862	◼◼	3045	888			
↙↙	645	273	◇◇	676	891			
⋈⋈	839	1086	⁒⁒	722	323			
++	772	259	◇◇	721	324			
UU	3348	264	◼◼	720	326			

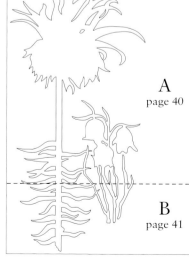

A page 40

B page 41

The chart for the 'Fritillaria' panel has been split over two pages. Refer to this diagram to check how the chart fits together.

41

Pear blossom

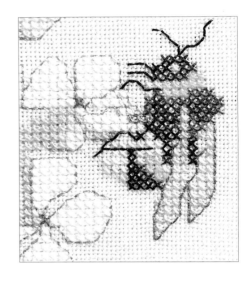

A PEAR TREE laden with blossom is one of the prettiest sights in spring. The fragile petals are a pale creamy white, almost transparent, yet when massed on the boughs they create a beautiful frothy cloud. In my garden there is an extremely old, tall pear tree and when it is in flower and the sun is shining I love to watch the bees busily flying from one scented blossom to another.

I thought it would be charming to decorate a tablecloth and napkins with this beautiful springtime design, which will bring a touch of the garden indoors and brighten your mealtimes whatever the weather. Adapt the size of the cloth to suit the size of your table. For a larger table, add more blossoms and bees to make the flower garland bigger and for a smaller table, reduce the number of motifs accordingly.

Pear blossom linen

Each of the blossom motifs measures
11.5 x 10cm (4¹/₂ x 4in)

YOU WILL NEED

28-count cream linen
FOR THE TABLECLOTH
180 x 175cm (71 x 69in)
FOR EACH NAPKIN
61.5 x 59cm (24 x 23in)
Stranded embroidery thread
as given in the key
No. 24 tapestry needle
Needle and sewing thread

THE TABLECLOTH

1 Prepare the linen as outlined on pages 138–140. Find the centre of the fabric and carefully mark the central vertical and horizontal lines with basting stitches. Measure 25cm (10in) from the centre of the fabric to each side and mark with a pin. This point is the inner edge of the body of the central bumble bee on each side. Begin stitching from this point.

2 With one strand of embroidery thread in the needle and following the chart, work each cross stitch over two threads of the fabric, ensuring that all the upper threads

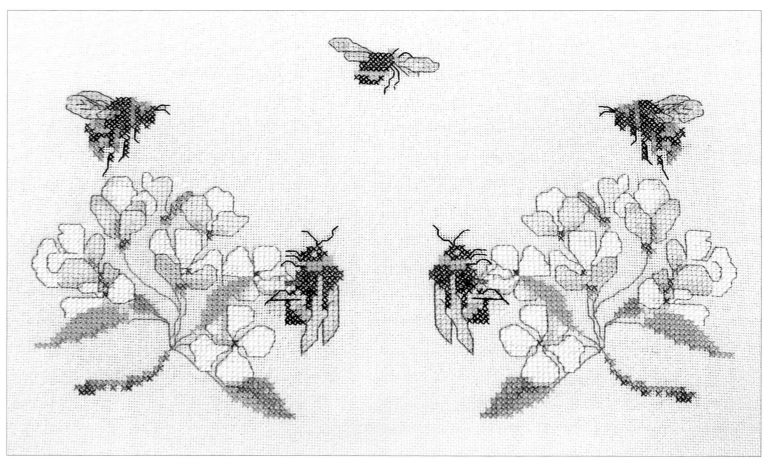

Tablecloth detail

of each stitch go in the same direction. To add definition to the blossom petals and the bees' wings, use two strands of thread in the needle over two threads of the fabric when working these details.

3 Follow the chart to complete the cross stitching; each square represents one stitch. Complete the back stitch details using one strand of embroidery thread in the needle, and referring to the key for colours of thread to be used.

THE NAPKIN

1 The napkins can be embroidered with either a bee or a blossom detail. To stitch a bee, follow the chart for the tablecloth. If stitching a blossom detail, follow the chart on page 47. Prepare the linen as outlined on pages 138–140. Find the centre of the linen and carefully mark the central vertical and horizontal lines with basting stitches.

2 To stitch a motif in the centre of the napkin, find the centre of the motif on the chart and begin stitching from this point, working from the centre of the linen. To stitch a motif in the corner of the napkin, measure 10cm (4in) along the bottom edge of the linen and 10cm (4in) up one side from a corner, then baste lines vertically and horizontally from these points; where the lines intersect is the centre of the corner motif. Begin stitching from this point.

3 With one strand of embroidery thread in the needle and following the appropriate

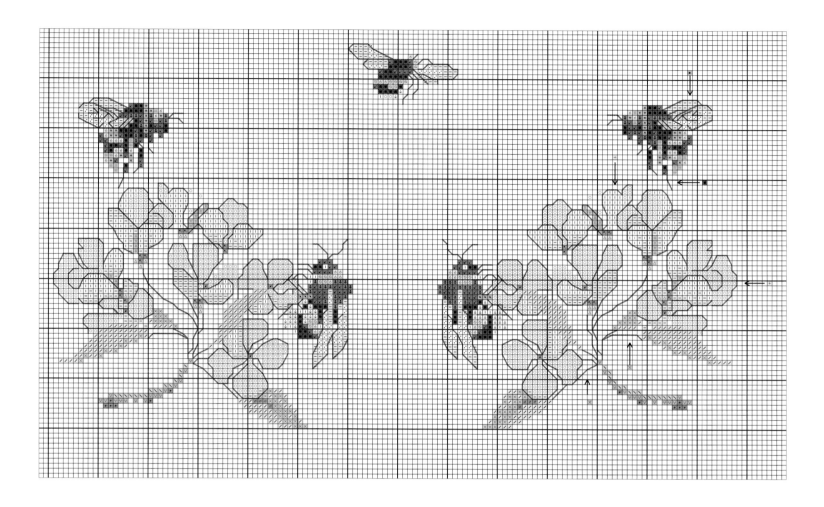

chart, work each cross stitch over two threads of the fabric, ensuring that the upper threads of each stitch are following the same direction. Use two strands of embroidery thread in the needle, over two threads of the fabric, when stitching the petals and bees' wings. Follow the chart to complete the cross stitching; each square of the chart represents one stitch.

4 Complete the back stitch details using one strand of embroidery thread in the needle, and referring to the key for the colours of thread to be used.

FINISHING

Remove the finished tablecloth or napkin from the hoop or frame and hand wash it carefully in warm water. When the embroidery is almost dry, lay it face down on a towel and press with a hot iron. To complete the 'Pear blosssom' tablecloth and napkins, hemstitch and fringe the edges as shown on page 142.

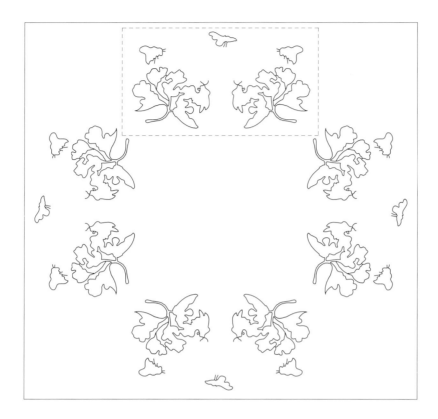

The chart on page 45
shows one section of
the 'Pear blossom'
tablecloth design.
Repeat this section
four times to complete
the tablecloth.

PEAR BLOSSOM TABLECLOTH *key*

	DMC	ANCHOR
○○ ○○	blanc #	2 #
⁄⁄	472	253
×× ××	471	265
‖ ‖ ‖ ‖	642	392
⚇⚇	469	267
\\ \\	3053	843
∅∅ ∅∅	470	266
↖↖	367	216
△△ △△	368	214
∴∴	822	390
– – – –	644	391
∨∨ ∨∨	3052	844
■■	3371	382
⚡⚡	3051	845
6 6 6 6	444	291
♪♪	433	358
‖ ‖	ecru	387
⊘⊘ ⊘⊘	725	305
↙↙	898	380
▲▲ ▲▲	762	234
⚇⚇	414	235
✳✳ ✳✳	783	307
‖‖ ‖‖	436	363
▲▲ ▲▲	640	393
++ ++	318	235

You will need two skeins of any thread marked #

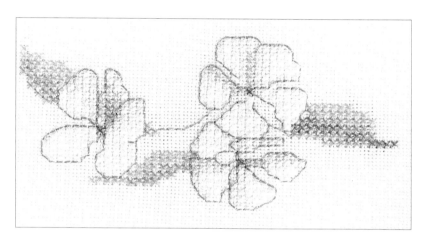

Napkin detail

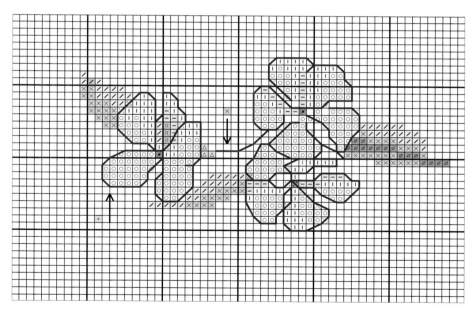

Follow this chart when stitching the blossom motif on a napkin. Follow the key shown on the left.

Crocus

CROCUSES APPEAR in bright drifts of colour in meadows and gardens at the end of winter, and as a result are often called the announcers of spring. They brave snow, frost and biting winds to poke their way out of the ground, heralding the start of warmer weather. When the sun is shining, they open up their petals fully as if to show off their flaming orange stamens, the stigmas of which are used to make saffron, the yellow flavouring and food colouring.

Crocuses look best *en masse*, either naturalized in grass or grown in tubs or pots. There are many types of crocus, ranging in colour from purple and yellow to white and pink. This panel shows some of the more common varieties. The dark purple crocuses are my favourite; it is their gleaming petals that makes them especially lovely.

Crocus panel

The finished design measures
43 x 11cm (17 x 4½in)

YOU WILL NEED

*36-count white linen,
approx. 50 x 18cm (19¾ x 7in)
Stranded embroidery thread as
given in the key
No. 24 tapestry needle
Strong board or card
Strong thread for lacing
Mount and frame of your choice*

THE EMBROIDERY

1 Cut the linen to the required size, bearing in mind the size of the frame that you will be using for this project. The amount suggested here will result in approximately 7cm (2¾in) of unstitched fabric all around the design.

2 Prepare the linen as outlined on pages 138–140. Find the centre of the fabric, then carefully mark the central vertical and horizontal lines with basting stitches.

3 Locate the centre of the 'Crocus' cross stitch chart and mark it for your reference.

Working with one strand of embroidery thread in the needle, begin stitching the design from this point, working each cross stitch over two threads of the fabric and ensuring that the upper threads of each stitch go in the same direction.

4 Follow the 'Crocus' chart to complete the cross stitching; each square of the chart represents one stitch.

5 Complete the back stitch details that edge each of the crocus flowers, using one strand of embroidery thread in the needle, and referring to the key for colours of thread to be used.

FINISHING

1 Remove the finished embroidery from the hoop or frame and hand wash it carefully in warm water. Then lay the embroidery face down on a towel and press with a hot iron until it is dry.

2 Choose a mount and frame that will co-ordinate with the colour in the 'Crocus' design and with your home furnishings. Cut a piece of board or card to fit the frame and then mount the embroidery as explained on page 141. Finally, set the mount in the frame.

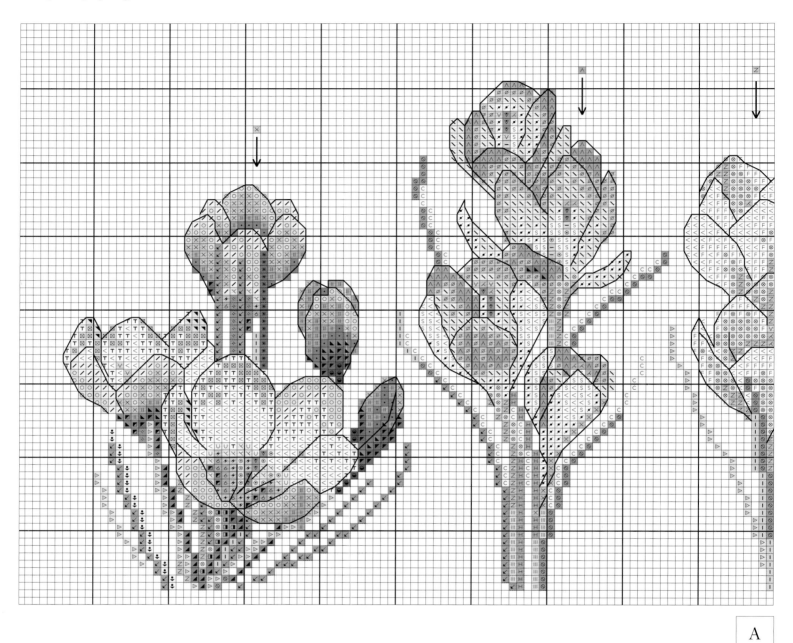

A

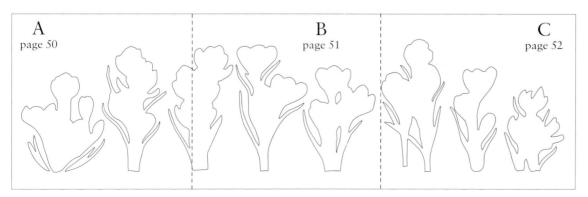

A
page 50

B
page 51

C
page 52

The chart for the 'Crocus' panel has been split over three pages. Refer to this diagram to check the relevant page on which each section of the chart falls.

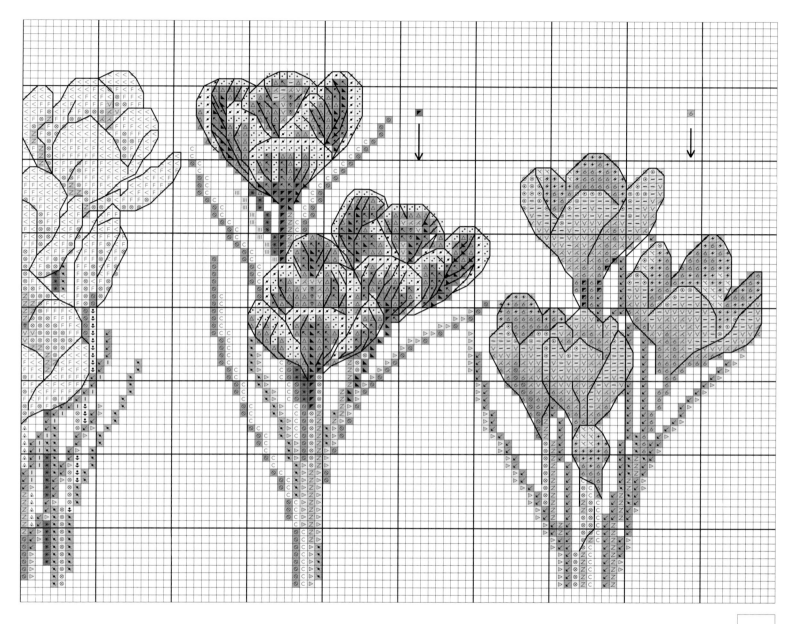

B

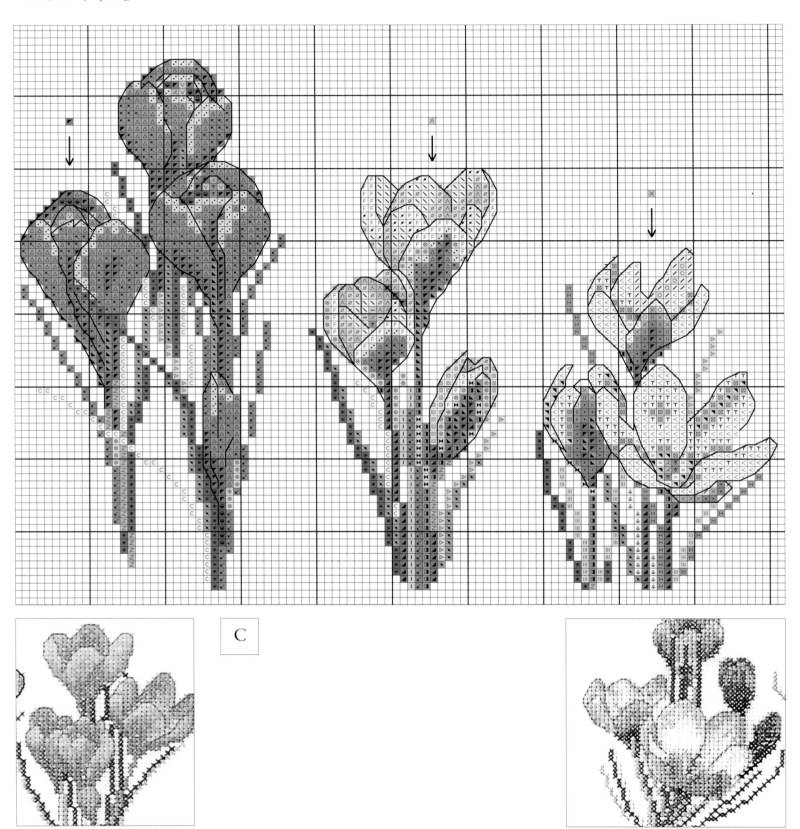

C

CROCUS PANEL *key*

	DMC	ANCHOR		DMC	ANCHOR
< < < <	blanc	2	III III III III	3348	264
H H H H	3347	266	✄ ✄	211	342
F F F F	822	390	\ \ \ \	210	108
⊗ ⊗ ⊗ ⊗	644	391	∅ ∅ ∅ ∅	209	109
Z Z Z Z	642	392	∧ ∧ ∧ ∧	208	110
▼ ▼ ▼ ▼	900	333	◤ ◤	327	101
S S S S	746	275	◥ ◢	550	101
C C C C	772	259	◥ ◥ ◥ ◥	552	99
◤ ◤ ◤ ◤	780	309	△ △ △ △	553	98
⬤⬤	823	152	∴ ∴	554	95
◪ ◪ ◪ ◪	3042	870	⊙ ⊙ ⊙ ⊙	743	302
▢ ▢ ▢ ▢	3041	871	– – – –	742	303
◢ ◢	3740	872	V V V V	741	304
▣ ▣ ▣ ▣	3743	869	⋋ ⋋ ⋋ ⋋	740	316
⁄ ⁄	3747	120	⋎ ⋎ ⋎ ⋎	3820	306
○ ○ ○ ○	341	117	⟋ ⟋	783	307
× × × ×	340	118	6 6 6 6	781	308
II II II II	3746	1030	⬩⬩	955	203
∴ ∴	333	119	I I I I	913	204
= = = =	744	301	⊙ ⊙ ⊙ ⊙	910	230
T T T T	762	234	⤡ ⤡	3818	923
⊠ ⊠ ⊠ ⊠	415	398	▴ ▴ ▴ ▴	369	1043
◥ ◥	318	235	▷ ▷ ▷ ▷	368	214
◈ ◈	839	1086	⬩⬩	320	215
U U U U	676	891	✳ ✳ ✳ ✳	319	1044

Romance of the rose

*For centuries the rose has been a symbol of love and beauty, and a source of inspiration
for painters, writers and musicians throughout the ages. From Roman times, when rose petals
were strewn on the floor to please emperors and their guests, to the present day when a Valentine's
gift of a red rose is a sign of love, the rose has earned its title of queen of the flowers.*

Romance of the rose
projects

ROSE BASKET PANEL

ROSE AND RIBBONS LINEN

ROSE AND BUD SAMPLER

THE ROSE has a long and fascinating history. The discovery of fossilized leaves suggests that roses were growing in the northern hemisphere about four million years ago, long before the existence of man. Excavations in Knossos, Crete, in the early 20th century revealed a fresco depicting cultivated roses, which proved that roses were being grown as early as 1800BC.

Roses are a recurring feature in Greek mythology. Aphrodite, the goddess of love, had her priestesses clothed in wreaths of white roses. Cleopatra was also a lover of scented roses. She decorated her palaces with these flowers and is said to have seduced Mark Antony in a throne room knee-deep in rose petals.

During the time of the Roman Empire roses became a symbol of lavish living. Horace, the Roman poet, noted that the fertile fields of Italy were being turned into rose gardens while olive trees were being neglected, and the economy was suffering as a result. Later, during the decline of the Roman Empire, the smell of roses in Rome was said to be overpowering.

By the Middle Ages, roses were grown in abundance throughout Europe. They were cultivated in the gardens of convents and abbeys for medicinal use, although their beauty and scent were also much admired. In the 19th century, roses were a feature of many royal gardens. Josephine, Empress of France from 1804 to 1809

planted a large collection of roses in the gardens of her château at Malmaison. This beautiful garden became one of the most famous rose gardens of its time, containing over 260 different varieties of rose. The garden was immortalized by the Belgian painter Redouté (1759–1840) in his painting *Jardin de Malmaison*, and was the forerunner of, and inspiration for, many contemporary rose gardens in all corners of the world. While in the past the rose was a flower for the pleasure of the nobility, it is now a flower that everyone can grow and enjoy.

Whether you prefer the old-fashioned wild dog roses, the delicate flowerheads of the climbing roses or the richly scented and petalled contemporary cultivated roses, most people will agree that the rose possesses the best combination of scent, colour and shape of all flowers. Year after year, varieties of rose flower in gardens

throughout the summer, producing more and more blooms, while other flowers have only a brief flowering season before dying. I am particularly fond of an old 'Peace' rose which I grow in my garden; it is pale yellow with pink blushed petals and has a lovely fragrance.

Roses also make wonderful cut flowers for arranging indoors. My favourite colour of rose for use in the home is yellow. I like to make simple table centre arrangements, but roses are very versatile: they can be wired into bouquets, garlands and swags, or used simply for decorative rose bowls. You can also dry roses and use the petals to make rose pot pourri and fill sachets and pillows with the scented mixture. Rose petals used to be thrown over the bride and groom at weddings, although now this tradition has been replaced in favour of tiny squares of coloured paper confetti, which I do not think have quite the same romantic quality!

An infusion of rose petals is added to many types of perfume, soap and bath lotions; and at one time even medicines were made from roses, although only rose-hip syrup is still produced today. If you ever desire to eat roses, it is possible to crystallize rose petals and decorate cakes

with them, although I must admit I have never tasted this delicacy.

I am content to enjoy the beauty of the rose and transform its complex structures into cross stitch designs. I find it particularly inspiring to study the work of artists who really mastered the art of painting roses well: Redouté, Hooker (1817–1911) and Von Spaendouck (1746–1822) are just a few whose work I especially admire.

I have selected a cross section of different rose designs to include in this chapter: a still-life design featuring an informal basket of newly picked roses, a botanical sampler featuring a number of varieties of rose, and a decorative rose and ribbon border design that can be altered to fit your requirements. I hope that you enjoy stitching them.

Rose basket

ONE OF the joys of growing roses is having a constant supply of blooms which can be cut either to make arrangements for the house or to make posies and bouquets for friends. This basket, overflowing with freshly-cut roses together with helenium and dill, creates a lovely composition of pinks, oranges and yellows, which I find very tranquil. My favourite are the old-fashioned roses, which to me are the essence of summer, with their pale pink petals and yellow stamens.

Although each flowerhead has only a brief flowering period before the petals fall, new flowers replace them to produce a consistently abundant display. Modern rose varieties might have more petals, a brighter colour and last longer, but somehow they lack the fragile beauty and perfume of the old-fashioned rose.

Rose basket panel

The finished design measures
33½ x 41cm (13½ x 16in)

YOU WILL NEED

*36-count white linen,
approx. 40.5 x 48.5cm (16 x 19in)
Stranded embroidery thread as
given in the key
No. 24 tapestry needle
Strong board or card
Strong thread for lacing
Mount and frame of your choice*

THE EMBROIDERY

1 Cut out the piece of linen, bearing in mind the amount you would like to remain visible between the stitched design and the frame. The amount suggested above will result in 7.5cm (3in) of unstitched linen all around the design.

2 Prepare the linen as outlined on pages 138–140. Find the centre of the fabric and carefully mark the central vertical and horizontal lines with basting stitches.

3 Find the centre of the chart and mark it for your reference. With one strand of

A

embroidery thread in the needle, begin stitching from this point, working each cross stitch over two threads of the fabric, and ensuring that all the upper threads of the stitch go in the same direction.

4 Follow the chart to complete the stitching; each square represents one stitch.

5 Complete the back stitch details using one strand of embroidery thread in the needle and referring to the key for colours of thread to be used.

FINISHING

1 Remove the finished embroidery from the hoop or frame and hand wash it in warm water. Then lay it face down on a towel and press with a hot iron until dry.

2 Choose a mount and frame to suit the colours in the design. Cut a piece of board or card to fit the frame and mount the embroidery as described on page 141. Set the mount in the frame.

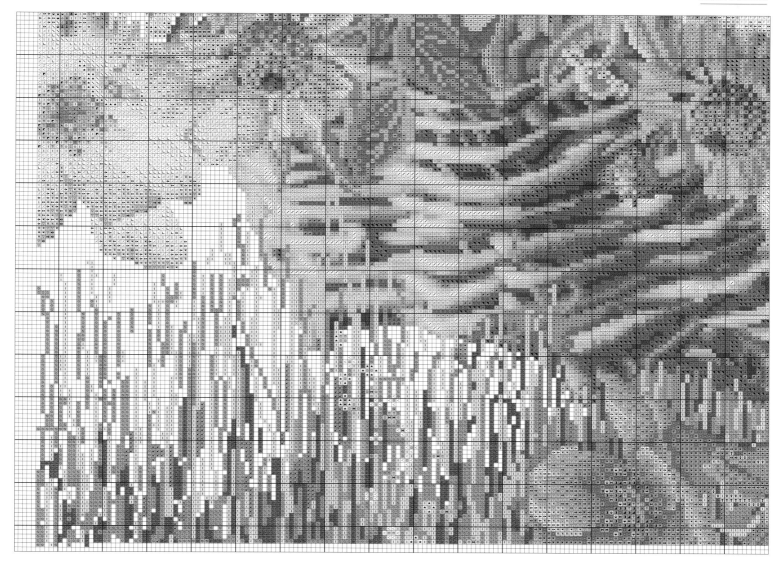

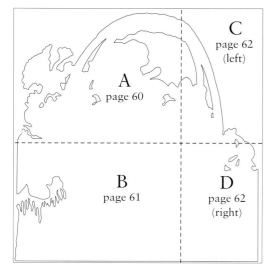

C
page 62
(left)

A
page 60

B
page 61

D
page 62
(right)

B

The chart for the 'Rose basket' panel has been split over three pages. Refer to this diagram to check the relevant page on which each section of the chart falls.

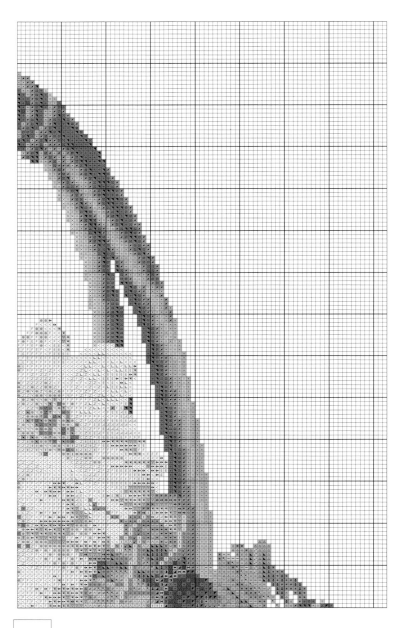

C

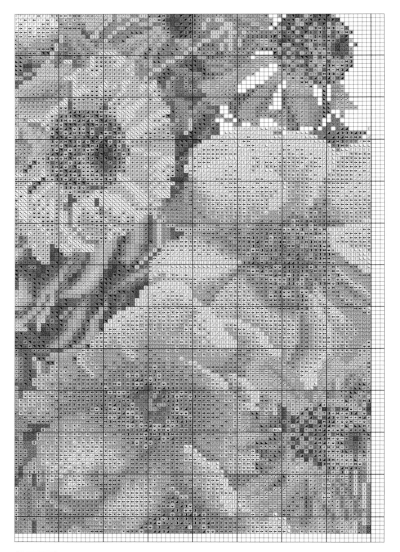

D

ROSE BASKET PANEL *key*

	DMC	ANCHOR		DMC	ANCHOR		DMC	ANCHOR
	445	288		740	316		372	887
	734	279		970	925		680	901
	3819	278		946	332		729	890
	444	291		900	333		975	357
	935	861		720	326		3826	1049
	469	267		721	324		976	1001
	470	266		722	323		3827	311
	471	265		3825	336		895	1044
	472	253		355	1014		3346	267
	3371	382		869	375		3347	266
	898	380		3051	845		3348	264
	801	359		3362	263		772	259
	433	358		3363	262		955	203
	434	310		3364	261		3046	887
	435	365		561	212		676	891
	436	363		562	210		677	361
	437	362		522	860		746	275
	738	361		524	858		3830	5975
	739	366		780	309		356	1013
	918	341		782	308		3778	1013
	920	1004		783	307		758	9575
	921	326		3822	295		3779	868
	922	1003		3820	306		945	881
	742	303		370	889		951	1010
	741	304		371	888		3770	1009

Rose and ribbons

THIS PRETTY design for a cushion and tablecloth features scrambling stems of tiny yellow rosebuds and foliage encircling a matching yellow ribbon. I have always loved climbing roses and find it fascinating how the little green tendrils wrap themselves around trellis and brickwork, finding nooks and crannies in the most unlikely of places. Climbing roses produce a wonderful display of colour in midsummer. Their dainty buds remain closed for days until one morning they suddenly burst open into a glorious mass of fluffy rosettes.

Inspired by a rose-framed cottage window, where on sunny summer days you can open the window and smell the sweet fragrance of flowers, this design allows you to bring a taste of summer into your house to brighten the winter months.

Rose and ribbons linen

The finished tablecloth design measures 55 x 55cm (21½ x 21½in);
the finished cushion design measures 45 x 45cm (18 x 18in)

YOU WILL NEED

Stranded embroidery thread as given in the key
No. 24 tapestry needle • Needle and thread

FOR THE TABLECLOTH
28-count white linen, approximately 134 x 134cm (53 x 53in)

FOR THE CUSHION
28-count white linen, approximately 53 x 53cm (21 x 21in)
Printed cotton fabric, 26 x 26cm (10½ x 10½in) • Pins
Linen backing fabric, 60 x 53cm (23½ x 21in)
Cushion pad, 50 x 50cm (19¾ x 19¾in) • 3 buttons

THE TABLECLOTH

1 Having chosen a piece of linen to fit your table, prepare as outlined on pages 138–140. Find the centre of the linen and carefully mark the central vertical and horizontal lines with basting stitches.

2 Measure 17.5cm (7in) from the centre of the fabric to each side and mark with a pin on each side. These points are the centre of the inner edges of the design, and this is where you start stitching.

3 Find the relevant point on the chart. As the design is symmetrical, the chart shows

only one corner of the design; each end of the chart is the centre of one side of the design. To stitch the whole design, simply work a mirror image of the chart to complete one half of the design, then repeat the process to work the second half.

4 With one strand of embroidery thread in the needle, begin stitching the design from this point, working each cross stitch over two threads of the fabric. Ensure that all the upper threads of the stitch go in the same direction. Follow the chart to complete the cross stitching; each square of the chart represents one stitch.

THE CUSHION

1 Prepare the fabric as outlined on pages 138–141. Find the centre of the fabric and carefully mark the central vertical and horizontal lines with basting stitches.

2 Measure 17cm (6³/4in) from the centre of the fabric to each side and mark with a pin on each side. These points are the centre of the inner edges of the design, and this is where you begin to stitch.

3 Find the relevant point on the chart. As the design is symmetrical, the chart shows only one corner of the design; each end of the chart is the centre of one side of the design. To stitch the whole design, simply work a mirror image of the chart to complete one half of the design, then repeat the process to work the second half.

4 With one strand of embroidery thread in the needle, begin stitching the design from this point, working each cross stitch over two threads of the fabric. Ensure that all the upper threads of the stitch go in the same direction. Follow the chart to

complete the cross stitching; each square of the chart represents one stitch.

FINISHING

1 Hand wash the finished embroidery in warm water. Lay it face down on a towel and press with a hot iron until dry. To finish the tablecloth, hemstitch and hem around all four edges following the instructions on pages 138–141.

2 To finish the cushion, first turn under the edges of the piece of printed cotton fabric by 1cm (³/8in) and press. Place the cotton face upwards in the centre of the embroidered linen. Pin and topstitch around the sides, approximately 2mm (¹/16in) from the edge. This piece will form the front of the cushion cover.

3 Cut the linen backing fabric into two pieces; the first piece should measure 33 x 36cm (13 x 14in), and the second 24 x 36cm (9¹/2 x 14in). Take the first piece of backing fabric and turn under one of its shorter ends by 4cm (1¹/2in). Pin and stitch about 3cm (1¹/4in) from the edge, then press. Take the second piece of backing fabric and turn under one of its shorter ends by 1.5cm (¹/2in), stitch and press.

4 Stitch up the cushion cover following the instructions on pages 138–141. Turn the cover the right side out through the back flap and add buttons for a decorative touch. Insert a cushion pad to complete.

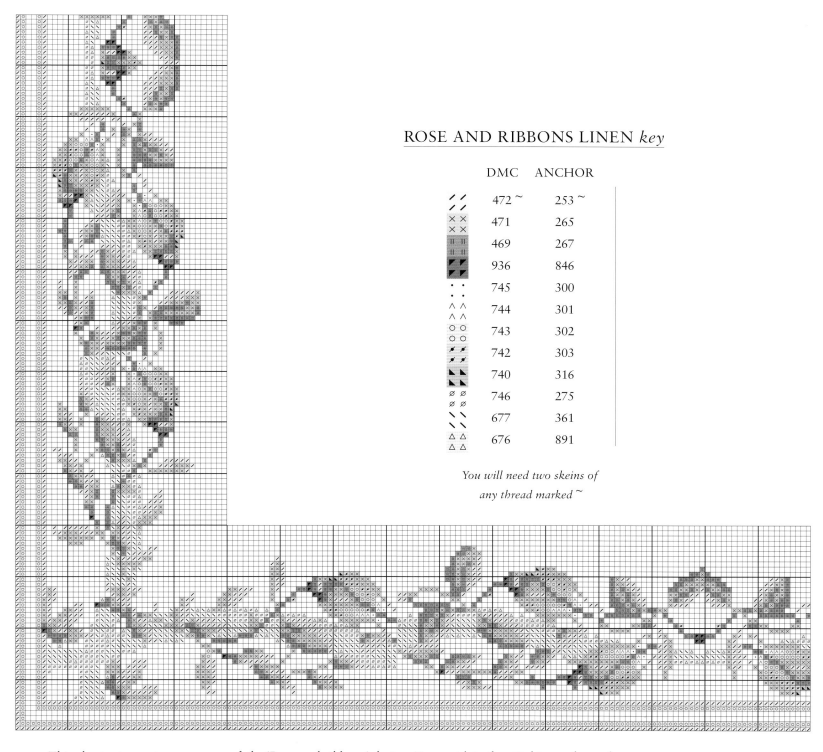

ROSE AND RIBBONS LINEN *key*

	DMC	ANCHOR
⁄ ⁄	472 ~	253 ~
× ×	471	265
‖ ‖	469	267
◣ ◣	936	846
· ·	745	300
∧ ∧	744	301
○ ○	743	302
◪ ◪	742	303
◥ ◥	740	316
ø ø	746	275
╲ ╲	677	361
△ △	676	891

You will need two skeins of
any thread marked ~

This chart represents one corner of the 'Rose and ribbons' design. To complete the stitching, refer to the instructions on page 66. A pretty alternative would be to repeat the rose pattern to the outside of the ribbon.

Rose and bud

R OSES ARE one of the most popular flowers grown today. There are so many varieties that you could devote your entire garden to roses, and still have plenty of colour from spring to autumn. This sampler illustrates just seven roses from the hundreds now grown. The 'Canary Bird' is a wild rose that blooms in the spring and its miniature flowers have a lovely fragrance. The cultivated 'Compassion' rose has wonderful apricot flowerheads and grows to a spectacular height.

In comparison, the 'Harriny' variety is delicate, but its coffee-coloured petals have a beautiful scent. The 'Sea Pearl' has gorgeous frilled petals, but only a subtle perfume. 'Dainty Bess', as its name suggests, is small, but its flowering season lasts all summer. Finally, the 'Golden Wings' rose produces a lovely display through the summer months.

Rose and bud sampler

The finished design measures
35 x 33.5cm (14 x 13½in)

YOU WILL NEED

36-count cream linen,
approx. 50 x 48.5cm (19¾ x 19in)
Stranded embroidery thread as
given in the key
No. 24 tapestry needle
Strong board or card
Strong thread for lacing
Mount and frame of your choice

THE EMBROIDERY

1 Cut out the fabric, bearing in mind the amount you would like to remain visible between the stitched design and the frame. The amount suggested above will result in approximately 7.5cm (3in) of unstitched fabric all around the design.

2 Prepare the fabric as outlined on pages 138–140. Find the centre of the fabric and carefully mark the central vertical and horizontal lines with basting stitches.

3 Find the centre of the chart and mark it for your reference. With one strand of

Rosaceae

Canary
Bird

Golden Wings

'Dainty Bess'

Compassion

Harriny

Sea Pearl

A

embroidery thread in the needle, begin stitching the 'Rose and bud' sampler from this point, working each cross stitch over two threads of the fabric, and ensuring that all the upper threads of the stitch go in the same direction. Follow the chart to complete the cross stitching; each square of the chart represents one stitch.

4 Complete the back stitch details using one strand of embroidery thread in the needle, and referring to the key for the colours of thread to be used.

FINISHING

1 Remove the finished embroidery from the hoop or frame and hand wash it in warm water. Then lay it face down on a towel and press with a hot iron until dry.

2 Choose a mount and frame to suit the design and your home furnishings. Cut a piece of board or card to fit and mount the embroidery as explained on page 141. Set the mount in the frame.

B

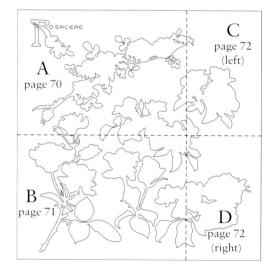

The chart for the 'Rose and bud' sampler
has been split over three pages. Refer to this
diagram to check the relevant page on
which each section of the chart falls.

71

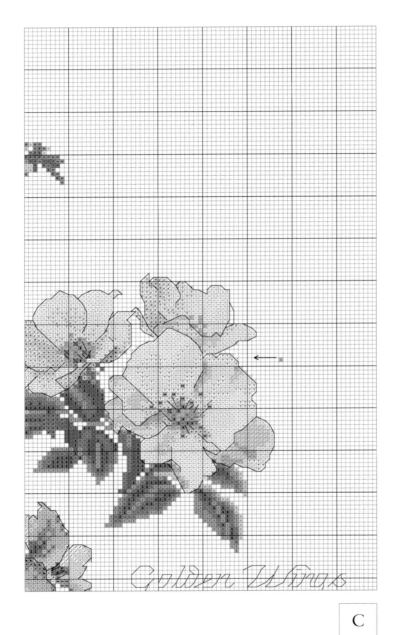

C

D

ROSE AND BUD SAMPLER *key*

	DMC	ANCHOR		DMC	ANCHOR		DMC	ANCHOR
	350	11	T T	677	361	V V	772	259
	815	44		437	362		754	1012
	369	1043		977	1002		310	403
	890	218		3827	311	E E	3777	1015
	319	1044		780	309	+ +	355	1014
	367	216		781	308	K K	3830	5975
	320	215	F F	782	307		356	1013
	368	214	C C	783	306		3778	1013
	838	1088	M M	642	392		758	9575
	839	1086	Z Z	644	391	– –	3779	868
	840	1084		680	901		347	1025
	934	862		729	890	L L	349	13
	936	846		3820	306		3801	1098
	580	924		3821	305	= =	3705	35
	581	281		3822	295	△ △	3706	33
Y Y	746	275		742	303		3708	31
	900	333		743	302		300	352
	720	326	S S	744	301		400	351
	721	324	H H	745	300	Ø Ø	301	1049
W W	722	323	< <	3823	386		3776	1048
	3825	336	▷ ▷	3011	856	∧ ∧	402	1047
	945	881	△ △	3012	855		326	59
4 4	951	1010		3013	853		309	42
♡ ♡	3340	329	▲ ▲	895	1044	· ·	961	76
N N	3341	328		3345	268	‖ ‖	962	75
3 3	3824	8		3346	267	× ×	3716	25
	3045	888	I I	3347	266	○ ○	963	23
U U	3046	887	6 6	3348	264	∕ ∕	819	271
	3047	852	> >	3819	278			

Herbal garden

There is something wonderfully traditional about a herb garden. Herbs have been
grown throughout history for their medicinal, culinary and aromatic uses. Nowadays,
although herbs are used mainly in the kitchen, they still provide lovely decorative foliage,
colourful flowers and superb fragrances and are an attractive feature in any garden.

Herbal garden projects

KITCHEN HERBS PANEL

CORNFLOWER TRAY CLOTH

GARDEN HERBS PANEL

I HAVE a little herb garden that I can see from my kitchen window, in which I grow parsley, thyme, mint and lavender. I like to use fresh herbs in my cooking as much as possible and enjoy being able to pick them straight from the garden.

The herb gardens of today are very different from those that were created in ancient Egypt and Rome, which were laid out geometrically in a very ornate style. Later, in medieval gardens, herbs were grown in complicated chequerboard patterns, each bed walled in by stones both to contain the herbs and to enable them to be reached and plucked without trampling the neighbouring plants. In the 19th century, informal cottage gardens replaced the more ornamental styles of herb garden, and herbs were grown among other flowers and vegetables in a fashion that many gardeners still like to reproduce today.

In the Middle Ages, herbs were categorized into four types: salad, sweet, simple and pot herbs. Salad herbs, which included chicory and lamb's lettuce, were eaten raw as vegetables; sweet herbs such as marjoram and thyme were used to flavour foods; simple herbs, such as lavender, hyssop and St John's wort, were grown for medicinal use, while the pot herbs consisted of what we now call green and root vegetables. Today, we use the term 'herbs' to refer mainly to those plants used for medicinal and culinary purposes.

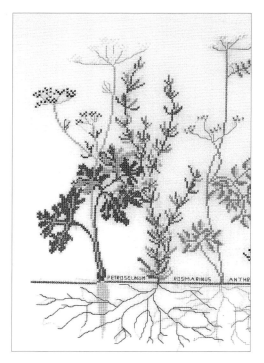

Herbal medicines were used to cure a variety of ailments, ranging from bronchitis to indigestion. They were taken in several forms, the simplest being an infusion or tea made from the leaves and flowers of a herb steeped in hot water. Natural herbal teas and medicines are still available from health food shops today.

Herbs have always been used in the kitchen and add flavour to any dish. In addition to their medicinal and culinary purposes, herbs also had many other uses in the home in the Middle Ages. They were strewn on the floor to disguise unpleasant smells, used in cosmetic ointments for the hair or skin and used as dyes for colouring wool and cotton. They were also dried to make pot pourri and the resulting scented mixture was used to fill sachets to perfume the home.

Nowadays herbs are often simply grown for their beautiful foliage and flowers, and make splendid additions to any flower bed. Fennel, for example, has fine feathery leaves and can be grown to provide a delicate lacy background to other plants. Angelica is grown for its spectacular purple stems and great stature, while variegated lemon balm provides a mass of lovely yellow and green leaves. Lady's mantle, with its pretty leaves and delicate green flowers, is often planted as a foil for brighter spring flowers, while the deep pink blooms of red valerian add splashes of bright colour to a flower bed.

Certain herbs can be used to create decorative borders along the edges of a pathway. Examples include lavender, with its dense compact bushes and fragrant lilac flowerheads, and sage with its grey felted leaves. Other herbal plants are grown as focal points in the garden: bay

trees can look very elegant when neatly clipped. Some herbs are grown for their wonderful scents, which are released when you brush past them. Mint and thyme are fragrant herbs, but you could choose chamomile, chives and lemon verbena which are also strongly scented.

Herbs grow well in containers, one advantage being that the container prevents the herbs taking over the flower bed. They also survive well when grown indoors on a windowsill. However, I prefer to see herbs growing naturally in the ground where they can gain nourishment from the soil and can benefit from the rain and sun throughout the year.

This chapter includes designs of some of my favourite herbs: a panel of culinary herbs for the kitchen, a cornflower tray cloth and a panel featuring a selection of some of the pretty herbs that can be found in the garden and in the wild.

Kitchen herbs

H ERBS HAVE been valued for hundreds of years for their culinary, medicinal and even dyeing properties. Some of the most common are featured here, from left to right, parsley, rosemary, chervil, chamomile, mint, dill, oregano and sage. These herbs are used in the kitchen to flavour casseroles, soups and stews; the leaves of some can also be infused to make herbal teas. All contain aromatic elements, and their intense flavour comes from bruising their leaves or stems. Because most herbs are used fresh, they make the dish not only more tasty but also more healthy.

Kitchen herbs are easy to grow in the garden – I grow mine in a flower bed near the kitchen door. They can also be grown in hanging baskets or tubs, or in pots on the kitchen windowsill and add colour and interest to any garden.

Kitchen herbs panel

The finished design measures
47.5 x 25cm (19 x 10in)

YOU WILL NEED

*36-count white linen,
approx. 63.5 x 40cm (25 x 16in)
Stranded embroidery thread
as given in the key
No. 24 tapestry needle
Strong board or card
Strong thread for lacing
Mount and frame of your choice*

THE EMBROIDERY

1 Cut out the linen, bearing in mind the amount you would like to remain visible between the design and the frame. The amount suggested will result in 7.5cm (3in) of unstitched fabric around the design.

2 Prepare the fabric as outlined on pages 138–140. Find the centre of the fabric and carefully mark the central vertical and horizontal lines with basting stitches.

3 Find the centre of the chart and mark it for your reference. With one strand of embroidery thread in the needle, begin

PETROSELNUM   ROSMARINUS   ANTHRISCUS   MATRICARIA   MENTHA   ANETHUM   ORIGANUM   SALVIA

stitching the design from this point. Work each cross stitch over two threads of the fabric and ensure that the upper threads of each stitch go in the same direction. Follow the chart to complete the stitching; each square represents one stitch.

4 Complete the back stitch details using one strand of embroidery thread in the needle, and referring to the key for the colours of thread to be used.

FINISHING

1 Remove the finished embroidery from the hoop or frame and hand wash it carefully in warm water. Then lay the embroidery face down on a towel and press with a hot iron until dry.

2 Choose a mount and frame that will co-ordinate with the colour in the 'Kitchen herbs' design and with your home furnishings. This design would look decorative in any kitchen or eating area. Cut a piece of board or card to fit the frame and mount the embroidery as explained on page 141. Set the mount in the frame.

KITCHEN HERBS PANEL *key*

	DMC	ANCHOR
	434	310
	890	890
	444	444
	445	288
	blanc	2
	3348	264
	3347	266
	3345	268
	472	253
	747	158
	519	1038
	793	176
	792	941
	895	1044
	3012	855
	3011	856
	818	23
	963	24

	DMC	ANCHOR
	3354	74
	738	361
	734	279
	732	281
	907	255
	905	257
	904	258
	400	351
	221	897
	831	277
	580	924
	912	209
	989	242
	955	203
	911	205
	702	226
	611	898
	367	216

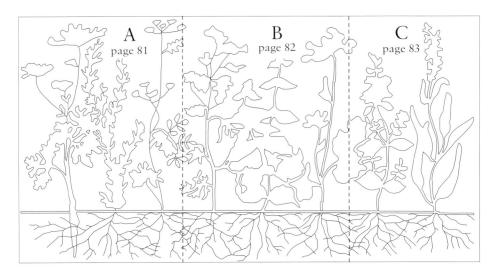

The chart for the 'Kitchen herbs' panel has been split over three pages. Refer to this diagram to check the relevant page on which each section of the chart falls.

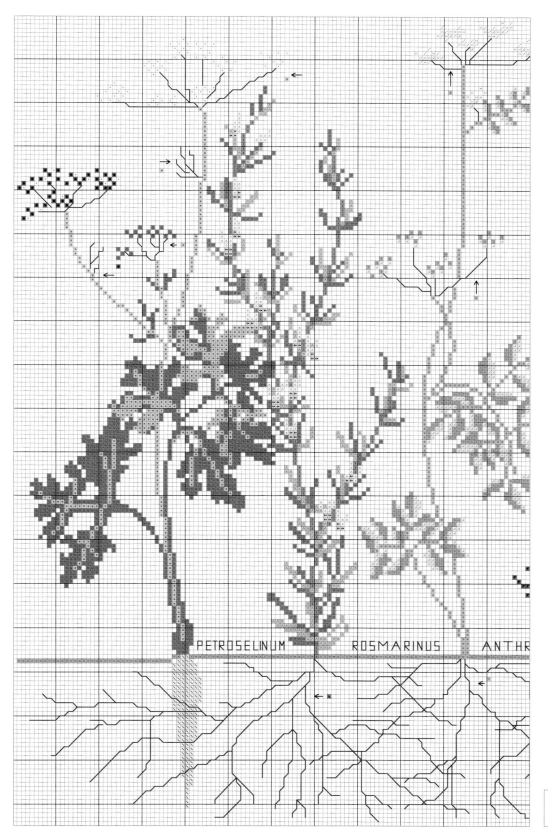

PETROSELINUM   ROSMARINUS   ANTHR

A

ISCUS   MATRICARIA   MENTHA   ANET

B

HUM   ORIGANUM   SALVIA

C

Cornflowers

THIS FRESH design was inspired by the sight of a field of golden-yellow ripe barley, decorated with a sprinkling of intense blue cornflowers. The whole field seemed to be waving and bending in the wind and all I could hear were the tops of the grain rustling and whispering. The cornflower is a wild flower with a brilliant colour, which seeds itself randomly, often in unexpected places. Cornflowers are also grown in gardens, where they create spots of colour among flowers in a border.

Although the design here is for a tray cloth, it could also be adapted to decorate a tablecloth and napkins. For a tablecloth, simply pick out some elements of the chart and stitch them randomly around the tablecloth fabric. To decorate plain napkins, stitch the cornflower motif in one corner of the piece of fabric.

Cornflower tray cloth

The finished design measures
25 x 19.5cm (10 x 7½in)

YOU WILL NEED

30-count white linen,
approx. 48 x 32.5cm (19 x 13in)
Stranded embroidery thread as
given in the key
No. 24 tapestry needle
Needle
Sewing thread

THE EMBROIDERY

1 Having selected a size to suit your tray, prepare the linen as outlined on pages 138–140. Find the centre of the fabric and carefully mark the central vertical and horizontal lines with basting stitches. Position the fabric so the two long sides are horizontal and the two short sides are vertical. The design will be stitched in the top right corner of the fabric.

2 Measure 5cm (2in) in from the right of the fabric and 9cm (3½in) up from the bottom. Where these measurements intersect is the base of the grain stem; this

CORNFLOWERS TRAY CLOTH *key*

is where you begin stitching. Find this point on the chart. With one strand of embroidery thread in the needle, begin stitching the design, working each cross stitch over two threads of the fabric and ensuring that all the upper threads of each stitch go in the same direction. Follow the chart to complete the cross stitching; each square of the chart represents one stitch.

3 Complete the back stitch details using one strand of embroidery thread in the needle, and referring to the key for colours of thread to be used.

FINISHING

1 Remove the finished embroidery from the hoop or frame and hand wash it in warm water. Then lay it face down on a towel and press with a hot iron until dry.

2 To complete the tray cloth, hemstitch the edges of the linen, following the instructions given on page 142.

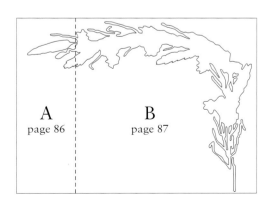

	DMC	ANCHOR
∕ ∕	800	144
○ ○	809	130
✕ ✕	799	145
‖ ‖	798	146
• •	797	132
◣ ◣	820	134
＼ ＼	993	1070
∅ ∅	992	1072
∧ ∧	3814	1074
◥ ◥	991	1076
◤ ◤	501	878
◄ ◄	502	877
△ △	503	876
⋰ ⋰	504	206
= =	677	361
◎ ◎	676	891
− −	729	890
∨ ∨	680	901
◄• ◄•	3829	901
■ ■	829	906
⋋ ⋋	834	874
⊘ ⊘	833	907
✦ ✦	832	888
♭ ♭	831	277
✿ ✿	830	277
⌙ ⌙	327	101
✕ ✕	3347	266
◤ ◤	3345	268

The chart for the 'Cornflower' tray cloth has been split over two pages. Refer to this diagram to check how the chart fits together.

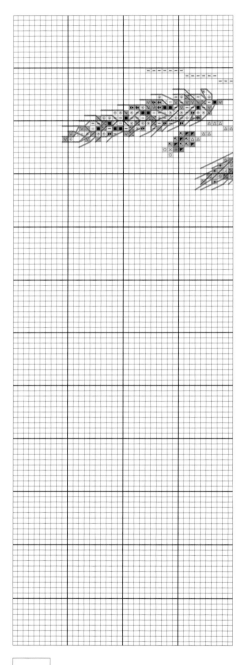

A

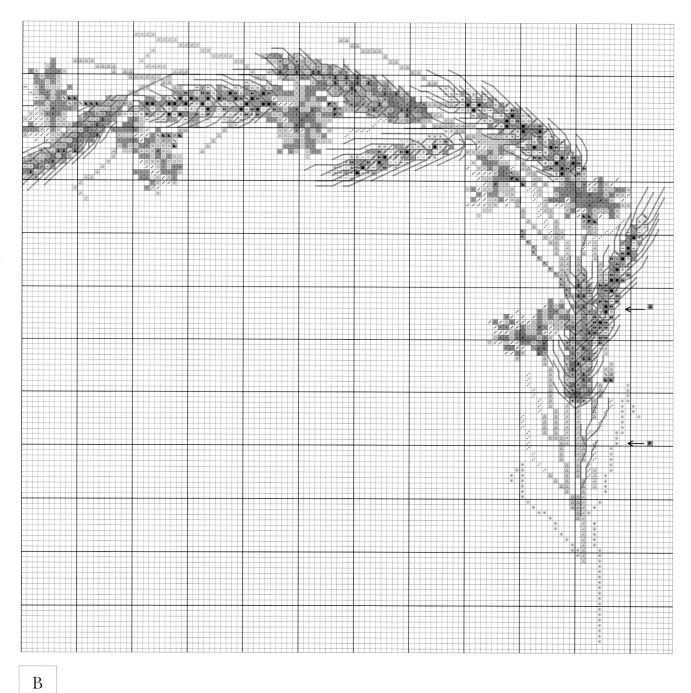

B

Garden herbs

THE HERBS featured in this panel all have valuable medicinal properties. Lady's mantle (*Alchemilla vulgaris*) not only provides an attractive edging for flower beds, it can also be used to ease indigestion. Borage (*Borago officinalis*), with its blue star-like flowers, can lift mild depression and reduce fever. Another herb with blue flowers, chicory (*Cichorium intybus*) can be used as a remedy for rheumatic twinges. Hops (*Humulus lupulus*) make an effective sedative, and can be used in a hop pillow.

Tansy (*Tanacetum vulgare*), an old cottage garden herb, was traditionally recommended for the treatment of scabies. The oil from St John's wort (*Hypericum perforatum*) provides relief for bruises and burns, while valerian (*Valeriana officinalis*) is a useful herbal tranquillizer for treating insomnia, anxiety or nervous exhaustion.

Garden herbs panel

The finished design measures
29.5 x 39cm (11½ x 15½in)

YOU WILL NEED

*36-count cream linen,
approx. 44.5 x 54cm (17½ x 21 in)
Stranded embroidery thread
as given in the key
No. 24 tapestry needle
Strong board or card
Strong thread for lacing
Mount and frame of your choice*

THE EMBROIDERY

1 Cut out the piece of linen, bearing in mind the amount you would like to remain visible between the stitched design and the frame. The amount suggested here will result in approximately 7.5cm (3in) of unstitched fabric all around the design.

2 Prepare the linen as described on pages 138–140. Find the centre of the fabric and carefully mark the central vertical and horizontal lines with basting stitches.

3 Find the centre of the chart and mark it for your reference. With one strand of

A

embroidery thread in the needle, begin stitching the 'Garden herbs' design from this point, working each cross stitch over two threads of the fabric, and ensuring that all the upper threads of the stitch go in the same direction. Follow the chart to complete the cross stitching; each square of the chart represents one stitch.

4 Complete the back stitch details using one strand of embroidery thread in the needle, and referring to the key for the colours of thread to be used.

FINISHING

1 Remove the finished embroidery from the hoop or frame and hand wash it in warm water. Then lay it face down on a towel and press with a hot iron until dry.

2 Choose a mount and frame to suit the colour in the design. Cut a piece of board or card to fit the frame and mount the embroidery as explained on page 141. Finally, set the mount in the frame.

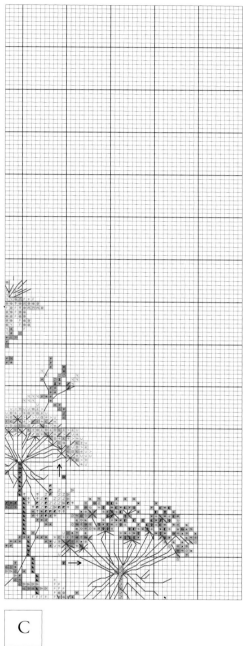

C

D

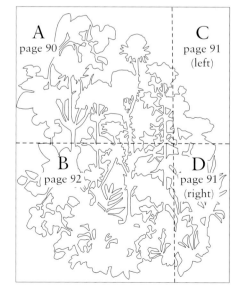

A
page 90

C
page 91
(left)

B
page 92

D
page 91
(right)

The chart for the 'Garden herbs' panel has
been split over three pages. Refer to this
diagram to check the relevant page on
which each section of the chart falls.

B

GARDEN HERBS PANEL *key*

	DMC	ANCHOR		DMC	ANCHOR		DMC	ANCHOR
	3807	122		3828	373		734	279
	792	941		869	375		640	393
	791	178		840	1084		642	392
	3689	49		839	1086		644	391
	3688	75		838	1088		822	390
	3687	68		327	101		580	924
	3803	69		356	1013		581	281
	3685	1028		355	1014		3819	278
	225	1026		3371	382		3021	905
	224	893		3379	868		3822	295
	223	895		3012	855		319	1044
	3721	896		3013	853		367	216
	775	128		3047	852		320	215
	3325	129		436	363		368	214
	3755	140		434	310		369	1043
	334	977		333	119		3051	845
	322	978		3746	1030		3052	844
	312	979		340	118		3053	843
	311	148		341	117		934	862
	603	62		3747	120		935	861
	601	63		3820	306		936	846
	600	59		3821	305		469	267
	504	206		782	308		470	266
	503	876		783	307		471	265
	502	877		740	316		472	253
	501	878		741	304		895	1044
	500	683		742	303		3345	268
	3773	1008		743	302		3346	267
	407	914		744	301		3347	266
	3772	1007		730	845		3348	264
	632	936		732	281		772	259
	819	271		733	280			

Wild flowers

*Many wild flowers are not only delicate but also extremely beautiful. It constantly amazes me
how these small flowers are able to flourish on the tiniest scrap of soil in the most impossible places,
such as in rock crevices or on hillsides and cliff faces, on old roofs and walls or on scrubby areas of
wasteland – and indeed anywhere else that their seed can find a place to germinate.*

Wild flowers projects

POPPIES PANEL

WILD PANSIES PANEL

MEADOW FLOWERS PANEL

HONEYSUCKLE CUSHION

WHEN WALKING in the countryside take time to stop and look carefully all
around and you will find many kinds of plants and flowers that you did
not know existed. Even in the garden, it is astonishing what you can find if you
look hard enough. When I lie down on my lawn in the summertime with my nose
almost touching the grass, I can see many miniature wild flowers in a variety of
colours – blue, white and pink – and many no larger than pinheads. It is at times
like these that I realize how miraculous nature is. I would love to embroider some
of these flowers, but they are so tiny that even one stitch would be too big for
them. So I limit my designs to wild flowers such as poppies and cornflowers,
which are more recognizable and large enough to see.

When I was young, I remember seeing drifts of ox-eyed daisies, cow parsley
and poppies growing in the grass at the sides of the roads, and they looked very
pretty stirring in the breeze as we drove past. There was a period when the local
authorities spent much time and money killing off the wild flowers, mistakenly
regarding them as weeds in an effort to 'tidy up' the roadsides. Now, after a swell
of popular support for the countryside in The Netherlands, as well as in many
other European countries, public opinion has forced a change of policy and the
growth of wild flowers is once again being actively encouraged.

Wild flowers are important not just because they add colour and beauty to the countryside. These plants also play a very important role in the environment and without them many insects, small animals and a host of microscopic creatures would become extinct as the plants provide much of their food. Now that there is an increased awareness of the role that wild flowers play, meadows, waysides, hedgerows and woodlands are also being re-planted, and public interest in wild-flower gardening is growing apace.

Growing wild flowers in the garden was once something that most people would have laughed at. But with these flowers gradually vanishing from the countryside, through a combination of modern farming methods and increased use of herbicides, growing your own wild flowers is a means of preserving them together with their ecology. You could transform a patch of your garden into a

wild flower meadow and grow blue corn-flowers, yellow corn marigolds, pink corn cockles and red poppies; in midsummer it would be a riot of colour. Alternatively, you could plant a whole border of wild flowers and grow mullein, larkspur, hyssop and foxgloves for a colourful grouping of purple and yellow.

Wild flowers can also be grown on a smaller scale if you prefer; a container on a patio or balcony planted with a selection of ox-eye daisies, cornflowers, harebells and field forget-me-nots would look very pretty. One advantage of growing wild flowers is that your garden will become a haven for bees, butterflies and birds, and you can be lulled by the gentle buzz of insects as you relax in the garden in the summer sunshine.

Of course, not everybody wants to grow wild flowers. Some would rather appreciate them in the countryside, in their natural habitats. Wild flowers can be

found everywhere – in shady woodlands, in meadows, along hedgerows and the edges of fields, and even at the seaside. When searching them out, look carefully because many flowers grow in the most unlikely places – hidden under leaves and fungi in woodlands, between bramble stems in hedgerows, in sand dunes and in rocky seaside cliffs. Because wild flowers are now protected, these plants should never be dug up. Nor is it wise to pick single flowers, as they never last for long if brought indoors. Be content to appreciate the flowers where they are, and leave them for others to enjoy too.

Each of the projects in this chapter is devoted to the beauty of wild flowers. They feature several of my favourite varieties of wild flower, including vibrant field poppies and fragrant honeysuckle. I hope that you will enjoy stitching some of these designs and that once your chosen embroidery is complete it will serve as a lasting reminder of the beauty of nature.

Poppies

T HE POPPY is one of the most instantly recognizable wild flowers and it is certainly my favourite. Bright red poppies can often be seen in summer, flowering along the sides of roads and fields. Unfortunately, they quickly droop if brought indoors, which is a good reason to let them grow naturally.

In my garden I have planted red and pink varieties of the cultivated poppy. When they open their papery petals and reveal their black centres, I regard it as a garden miracle. My one regret is that the flowers only bloom for a few days each year. Perhaps I should take a day off work during that time and sit in the garden for the whole day, simply soaking up their splendour. This stitched panel will serve as a vivid reminder of the beauty of poppies through the rest of the year.

Poppies panel

The finished design measures
21 x 21cm (8½ x 8½in)

YOU WILL NEED

30-count white linen,
approx. 28.5 x 28.5cm (11 x 11in)
Stranded embroidery thread
as given in the key
No. 24 tapestry needle
Strong board or card
Strong thread for lacing
Mount and frame
of your choice

THE EMBROIDERY

1 Cut out the fabric, bearing in mind the amount you would like to remain visible between the stitched design and the frame. The amount suggested for this project will result in about 7.5cm (3in) of unstitched fabric all around the design.

2 Prepare the fabric as outlined on pages 138–140. Find the centre of the fabric and carefully mark the central vertical and horizontal lines with basting stitches.

3 Find the centre of the chart and mark it for your reference. With one strand of

embroidery thread in the needle, begin
stitching the design from this point,
working each cross stitch over two
threads of the fabric. Ensure that all
the upper threads of each stitch go in
the same direction.

4 Follow the 'Poppies' chart to complete
the cross stitching; each square of the
chart represents one stitch.

FINISHING

1 Remove the finished embroidery from
the hoop or frame and hand wash it
carefully in warm water. Then lay the
embroidery face down on a towel and
press with a hot iron until dry.

2 Choose a mount and frame that will
co-ordinate with the colours in the
'Poppies' design and with your home
furnishings. Cut a piece of board or card
to fit the frame, then mount the finished
embroidery as explained on page 141.
Set the mount in the frame.

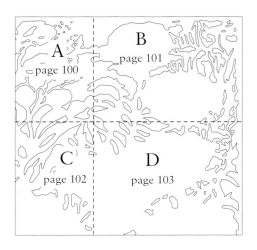

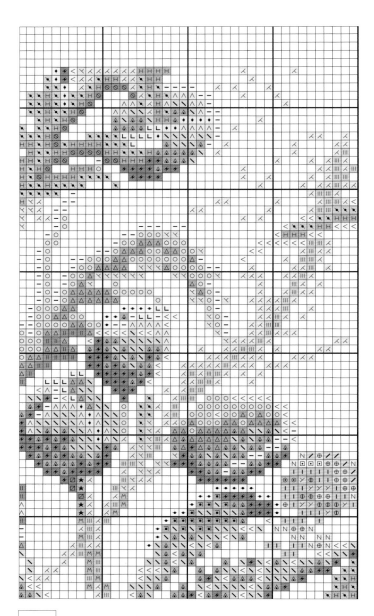

A

*The chart for the 'Poppies' panel has
been split over four pages. Refer to this
diagram to check the relevant page
on which each section of the chart falls.*

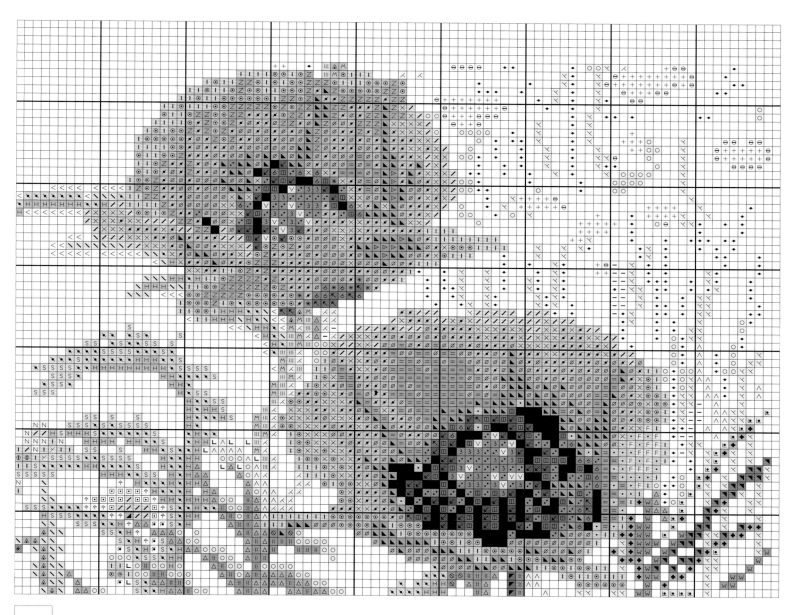

B

POPPIES *key*

	DMC	ANCHOR
	310	403
	741	304
	971	316
	368	214
	367	216
	351	10
	947	330
	503	876
	946	332
	966	240
	900	333
	319	1044
	902	897
	320	215
	327	101
	606	334
	721	324
	369	1043
	3042	870
	524	858
	890	218
	3348	264
	501	878
	3685	1028
	500	683
	722	323
	987	244
	823	152
	502	877
	920	1004
	989	242
	3721	896
	523	859

	DMC	ANCHOR
	988	243
	522	860
	504	206
	352	9
	720	326
	986	246
	471	265
	402	1047
	3045	888
	699	923
	561	212
	700	228
	blanc	2
	3046	887
	3047	852
	991	1076
	743	302
	701	227
	3740	872
	976	1001
	977	1002
	562	210
	782	308
	745	300
	563	208
	726	295
	762	234
	472	253
	772	259
	972	298
	307	289
	839	1086
	550	101
	841	1082

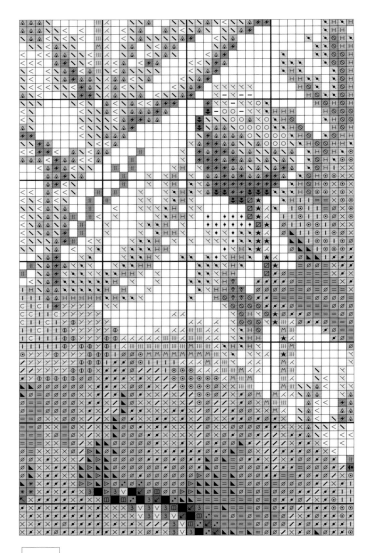

C

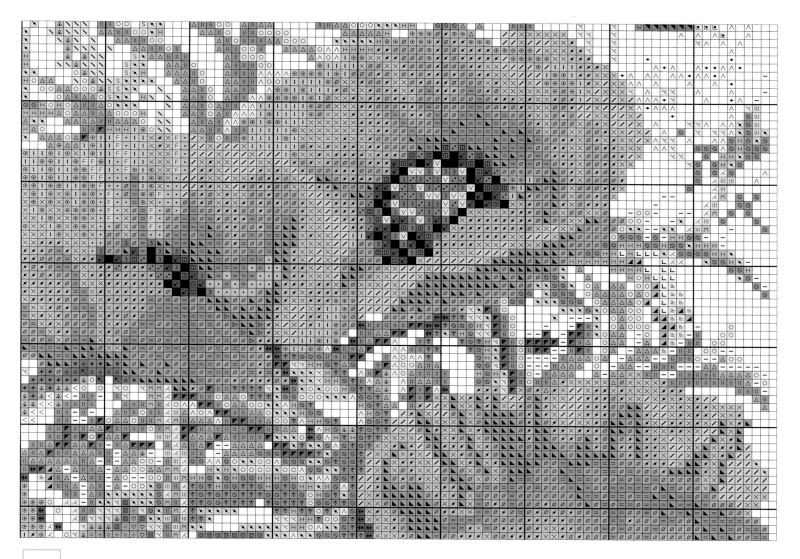

D

Wild pansies

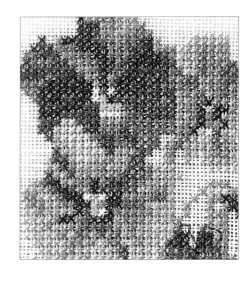

MEMBERS OF the Viola family, pansies can be found growing in moderate climates all over the world. Wild pansies are small and dainty and, with the distinctive markings on their petals, they sometimes look like they have faces. If you plant pansies in the garden they will grow back year after year, displaying a beautiful array of purple and blue. Pansies also look lovely growing in pots and baskets.

Pansies have long been popular flowers, and have provided inspiration for painters and poets throughout the centuries. The Victorians in 19th-century England were particularly fond of pansies. Many hybrids were created at this time by crossing different varieties of pansies. Exhibitions and conferences on the subject of pansies were held, and everything possible was decorated with pansy motifs.

Wild pansies panel

The finished design measures
37 x 19cm (14½ x 7½in)

YOU WILL NEED

*32-count cream linen,
approx. 52 x 34cm (20½ x 13¾in)
Scissors
Stranded embroidery thread
as given in the key
No. 24 tapestry needle
Strong board or card
Strong thread for lacing
Mount and frame of your choice*

THE EMBROIDERY

1 Prepare the piece of linen for working by cutting out the required amount, bearing in mind the amount you would like to remain visible between the stitched design and the frame. The size of fabric suggested for this project will result in approximately 7.5cm (3in) of unstitched fabric all around the design.

2 Prepare the piece of fabric for working as described on pages 138–140. Then find the centre of the fabric in order to mark the central vertical and horizontal lines with basting stitches.

3 Working with one strand of embroidery thread in the needle, begin stitching the design from this central point, working each cross stitch over two threads of the fabric. Ensure that the upper threads of each stitch go in the same direction.

4 Follow the 'Wild pansies' chart on the following pages to complete the stitching; each square represents one stitch.

5 Finally, complete the back stitch details, using one strand of embroidery thread in the needle and referring to the key for colours of thread to be used.

FINISHING

1 When the 'Wild pansies' embroidery is complete, remove the finished piece from the hoop or frame and hand wash it carefully in warm water.

2 When the embroidery is nearly dry, lay it face down on a towel and press gently with a hot iron until dry.

3 Choose a mount and frame that will co-ordinate with the colours in the 'Wild pansies' design and also with the colours of the room where the framed embroidery is to be displayed. Cut a piece of board or card and mount the embroidery, as described on page 141. Finally, set the mount in the frame.

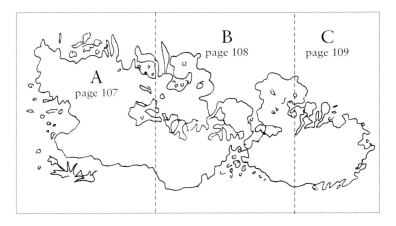

The chart for the 'Wild pansies' panel has been split over three pages. Refer to this diagram to check the relevant page on which each section of the chart falls.

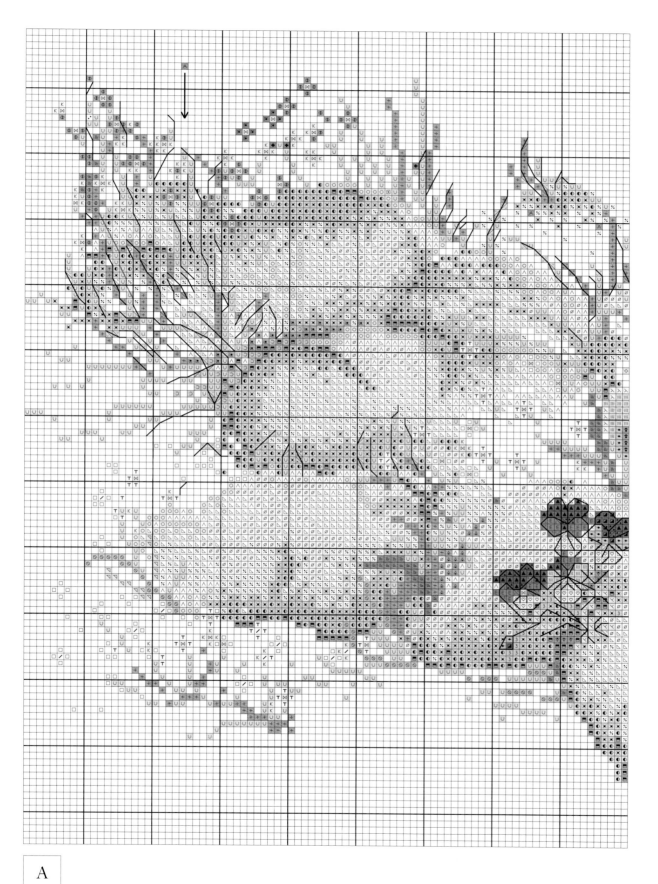

A

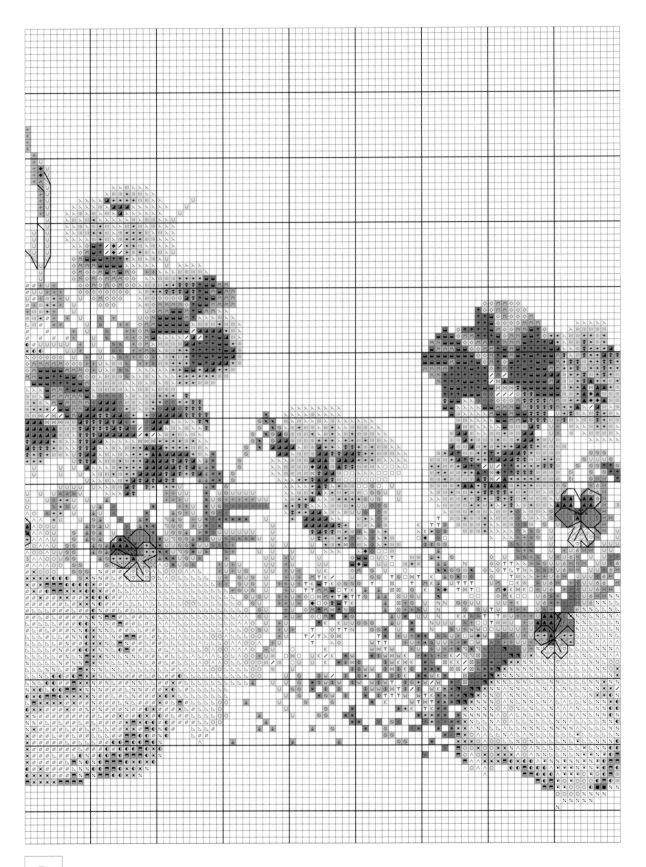

B

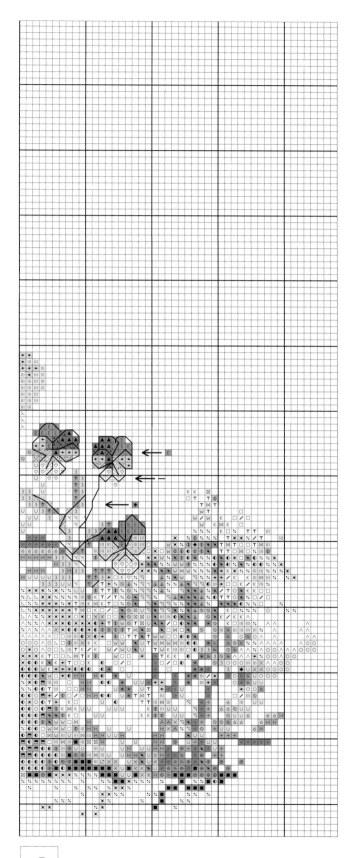

WILD PANSIES *key*

	DMC	ANCHOR		DMC	ANCHOR
	798	146		841	1082
	895	1044		3746	1030
	772	259		340	118
	3051	845		840	1084
	334	977		3756	1037
	3747	120		950	4146
	842	1080		524	858
	3755	140		3041	871
	3325	129		792	941
	3345	268		414	235
	3346	267		318	235
	3347	266		794	175
	3348	264		791	178
	322	978		368	214
	775	128		648	900
	543	933		blanc	2
	3770	1009		327	101
	793	176		520	862
	341	117		3072	397
	470	266		333	119
	986	246		740	316
	987	244		444	291
	988	243		550	101
	989	242		831	277
	471	265		833	874
	839	1086		310	403
	822	390		472	253
	762	234		905	257
	436	363		552	99
	644	391		744	301
	746	275		907	255

C

Meadow *flowers*

T HIS PANEL features a selection of pretty wild flowers in an attractive range of colours: a yellow buttercup, pink clover, blue cornflower, golden meadow grass and an orange-red poppy. To walk on a sunny summer day through a meadow where all these flowers were growing would be my idea of heaven.

The buttercup comes from a family with hundreds of varieties, and I think its petals really do shine like butter in the sunshine. Clover is a deliciously sweet-scented flower, a favourite with bees. The blue-petalled flower is a cornflower, of which there are over 500 varieties. I have included meadow grass in this design because it frequently grows among wild flowers in meadowland. The final flower is the poppy, my favourite wild flower, with its bright papery leaves and slender stem.

Meadow flowers panel

The finished design measures
27 x 23.5cm (10½ x 9in)

YOU WILL NEED

*36-count white linen,
approx. 42 x 38.5cm (16½ x 15in)
Stranded embroidery thread
as given in the key
No. 24 tapestry needle
Strong board or card
Strong thread for lacing
Mount and frame
of your choice*

THE EMBROIDERY

1 Cut out the linen, bearing in mind the amount you would like to remain visible between the stitched design and the frame. The amount suggested here will result in about 7.5cm (3in) of unstitched fabric all around the design.

2 Prepare the fabric as outlined on pages 138–140. Find the centre of the fabric and carefully mark the central vertical and horizontal lines with basting stitches.

3 Find the centre of the chart and mark it for your reference. With one strand of

embroidery thread in the needle, begin
stitching the design from this point,
working each cross stitch over two threads
of the fabric, and ensuring that the upper
threads of each stitch are following the
same direction.

4 Follow the 'Meadow flowers' chart to
complete the cross stitching; each square
of the chart represents one stitch.

5 Complete the back stitch details using
one strand of embroidery thread in the
needle, and referring to the key for colours
of thread to be used.

FINISHING

1 Remove the finished 'Meadow flowers'
embroidery from the hoop or frame and
hand wash it carefully in warm water.
When nearly dry, lay it face down on a
towel and press with a hot iron.

2 Choose a mount and frame that will
co-ordinate with the colours in the
'Meadow flowers' design and the room
where the embroidery is to be displayed.
Cut a piece of board or card to fit the
frame and mount the embroidery, as
explained on page 141. Finally, set the
mount in the frame.

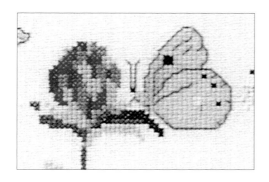

MEADOW FLOWERS *key*

	DMC	ANCHOR		DMC	ANCHOR
	310	403		504	206
	800	144		502	877
	742	303		915	1029
	503	876		938	381
	677	361		307	289
	801	359		445	288
	741	304		745	300
	319	1044		471	265
	809	130		469	267
	612	832		433	358
	3371	382		993	1070
	924	851		3348	264
	823	152		991	1076
	798	146		731	281
	368	214		444	291
	501	878		783	307
	820	134		738	361
	blanc	2		414	235
	320	215		733	280
	729	890		436	363
	367	216		935	861
	611	898		898	380
	606	334		720	326
	890	218		721	324
	831	277		722	323
	605	1094		3825	8
	603	62		822	390
	600	59		644	391
	369	1043		ecru	387
	725	305		762	234

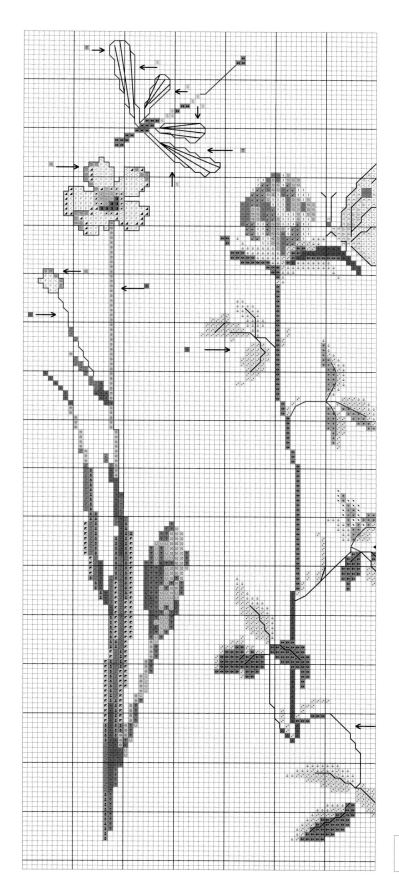

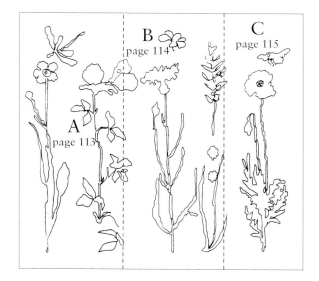

B
page 114

C
page 115

A
page 113

The chart for the 'Meadow flowers' panel
has been split over three pages. Refer to
this diagram to check the relevant page
on which each section of the chart falls.

A

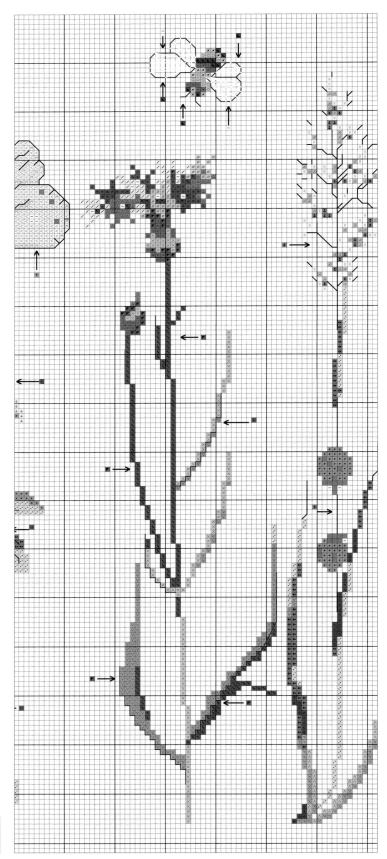

B

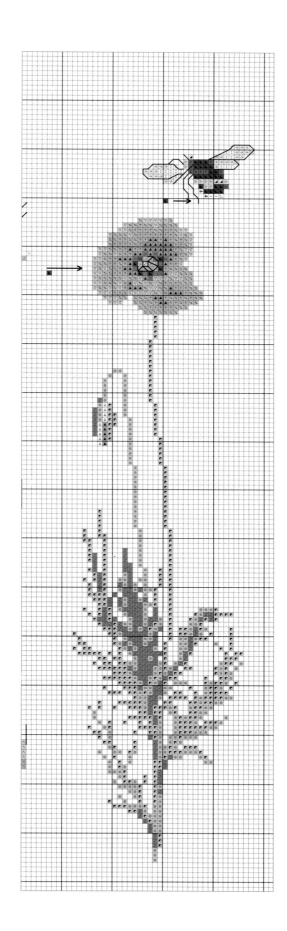

C

Honey suckle

THROUGHOUT THE summer months, honeysuckle can often be seen growing along garden walls, fences and trellises, its twisting stems and foliage supporting clusters of long-petalled flowers in shades of pink and yellow. There are many different varieties of honeysuckle, which flower at different times during the summer, but all of them have a sweet fragrance. On a late, still summer evening I like to sit outdoors with my eyes closed, where I can breathe in the delicious fragrance of the pale yellow honeysuckle growing in my garden.

In addition to its lovely scented flowers, honeysuckle produces another surprise later in the year – a display of glossy red berries. These berries brighten the garden as the flowers die down, as well as providing a source of food for the birds.

Honeysuckle cushion

The finished design measures
34 x 24cm (13³/₄ x 9¹/₂in)

YOU WILL NEED

36-count white linen,
approx. 46 x 36cm (18 x 14in)
Stranded embroidery thread
as given in the key
No. 24 tapestry needle
Sepia linen backing fabric
Needle, pins and thread
3 buttons
Cushion pad

THE EMBROIDERY

1 Cut out the required amount of fabric, then prepare it as outlined on pages 138–140. Find the centre of the piece of fabric and carefully mark central vertical and horizontal lines with basting stitches.

2 Find the centre of the honeysuckle cross stitch chart and mark it for your reference. With one strand of embroidery thread in the needle, begin stitching the design from this point, working each cross stitch over two threads of the fabric, and ensuring that all the upper threads of each stitch go in the same direction. Follow the chart to

complete the cross stitching; each square of the chart represents one stitch.

3 Complete the back stitch details as indicated on the chart. Use one strand of embroidery thread in the needle, and refer to the key for colours of thread to be used.

FINISHING

1 When the stitching is complete remove the embroidery from the hoop or frame and hand wash it in warm water. Then lay the embroidery face down on a towel and press with a hot iron until dry.

2 To complete the cushion, cut the sepia linen backing fabric into three pieces. The first piece should measure 46 x 36cm (18 x 14in), the second 33 x 36cm (13 x 14in) and the third 24 x 36cm (9½ x 14in).

3 Turn under the edges of the piece of embroidery and press. Place face upwards in the centre of the largest piece of backing fabric. Pin and topstitch around the edges, about 2mm (¹/₁₆in) from the edge.

4 Take the second largest piece of backing fabric and turn under one of its shorter

ends by 4cm (1½in). Pin and stitch this 3cm (1¼in) from the edge, then press.

5 Take the third piece of backing fabric and turn under one of its shorter ends by 1.5cm (½in), stitch and press.

6 Stitch up the 'Honeysuckle' cushion cover following the instructions on pages 141–142. Turn the cover right side out through the opening, then add buttons. Finally, insert a cushion pad – for a project of this size, use a pad measuring 44 x 34cm (17 x 13½in).

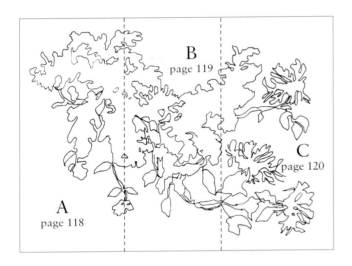

The chart for the 'Honeysuckle' cushion
has been split over three pages. Refer to
this diagram to check the relevant page
on which each section of the chart falls.

A

B

C

HONEYSUCKLE CUSHION *key*

	DMC	ANCHOR		DMC	ANCHOR
■ ■	310	403	◤ ◤	781	308
R II	986	246	U U	3031	905
◤ ◤	935	861	K K	3688	75
△ △	3053	843	⊩ ⊩	368	214
∴	320	215	E E	733	280
V V	369	1043	L L	840	1084
◀ ◀	839	1086	W W	841	1082
✕ ✕	3371	382	N N	734	279
6 6	989	242	3 3	772	259
✦ ✦	838	1088	⋋ ⋋	434	310
I I	3685	1028	⊕ ⊕	435	365
⊘ ⊘	471	265	✚ ✚	829	906
↙ ↙	3051	845	▪ ▪	758	9575
▲ ▲	469	267	4 4	727	293
▷ ▷	472	253	⊖ ⊖	356	1013
▪ ▪	3350	77	> >	351	10
✳ ✳	3052	844	▲ ▲	731	281
III III	436	363	◆ ◆	350	11
H H	581	281	⊕ ⊕	319	1044
M M	680	901	▢ ▢	3689	49
F F	580	924	⊡ ⊡	304	19
⊗ ⊗	783	307	◨ ◨	816	43
S S	726	295	★ ★	902	897
T T	725	305	◆ ◆	801	359
			+ +	372	887

Orchard harvest

I always think that autumn is a nostalgic time of year, when the long days of summer are coming to an end, the air is crisper and the cold of winter is waiting in the wings. Although the leaves on the trees are dying, they do so in a spectacular blaze of colour – a wonderfully rich combination of glorious golden browns, fiery reds, russets and mellow oranges.

Orchard harvest
projects

SEPTEMBER PLUMS PANEL

BILBERRIES PANEL

APPLES BOX

MOST OF the summer flowers have finished blooming by this time, leaving only the yellow and gold chrysanthemums, the Michaelmas daisies, and the autumn crocuses and cyclamens to carry on for a few more weeks before they too begin to droop. Stems are turning brown, branches are gradually becoming visible again, the sun is sinking lower in the sky and there is a hint of chill in the air and a crunch underfoot, sure signs that winter is on its way. Yet the one aspect of this time of year that I really look forward to is the fruit harvest. Suddenly, everywhere you look, fruit is ripening in the trees and on bushes. Cherries, apples, pears, plums, rhubarb, nuts and woodland fruits are all ready to be picked, and there is a heavenly, fruity scent in the air.

Strawberries are ready first, in the last weeks of summer and who can resist their sweet taste with a dollop of cream. We always used to grow strawberries in our garden when I was a child and I remember creeping under the strawberry nets to pick them, and getting caught by the buttons on the back of my dress. Apples are much easier to scrump, and they are also much easier to carry around with you when you are out playing for an afternoon. There is only one tree left in the garden where I grew up – a pear, called 'Claps favourite'. Although it is now really gnarled and old, it continues to produce wonderful fruit year after year.

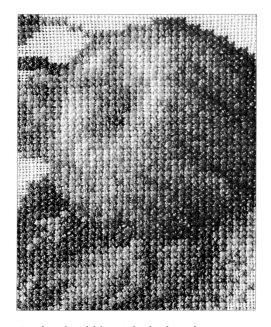

Apples should be picked when they part easily from the branch. Then they can either be eaten straight away, or stored for several months in a dry, frost-free place, such as a cellar or loft; even after storing, they still taste so much more delicious than those bought in the shops. Home-grown pears do not keep as long as apples once harvested and need to be eaten within a few weeks. My mother was a very good cook and used to preserve pears for the winter; these were then served with vanilla sauce.

Succulent plums were another favourite in our household when I was growing up. We always used to get our plums from my aunt, who had a lovely big plum tree in her garden. Sweet red cherries unfortunately never made it to the kitchen when I was young. They were so delicious, we used to eat them straight from the branch, provided the birds did not get

them first. Rhubarb was another fruit we used to grow and I still do today. I like to make rhubarb jam from my crop, but it is also lovely when baked in a pie.

In addition to harvesting the fruit in the garden, my sisters, brothers and I would go blackberry picking along the hedgerows near our village. Blackberries grew there in abundance before the advent of herbicides and we would collect a bumper crop each year. We would be armed with buckets and bags in which to collect the fruit and, by the end of the afternoon, we would be tired and aching from stretching for the higher berries, our arms, legs and faces would be scratched all over from the sharp thorns, and our faces and tongues would be purple with blackberry juice. However, we would have stripped the bushes bare and collected enough berries to feed the entire village. My mother would then make a delicious

blackberry juice, as well as blackberry pie and summer pudding with our store, so it was definitely worth the effort.

Once the excitement of harvesting the fruit was over, then it was time for cooking. I can still remember the enticing smells emanating from the kitchen. In addition to preserving pears and making jams and juices, my mother made many delicious desserts, including such favourites as apple pie, plum crumble, blackberry cobbler and rhubarb pie. Nowadays I do not cook so much and prefer to eat my fruit fresh from the fruit bowl, but when I was young, it always seemed to taste so much better in a pie.

In this chapter I have included some mouthwatering pictures of orchard fruits to stitch: succulent September plums ready for plucking, tiny blue bilberries still on the branch, and sweetly scented golden-red autumn apples.

September plums

ONE OF the blessings of late summer is the promise of a bumper harvest of plums. These delicious fruit hold a special memory for me. When I was young, my sister and I used to stay with an aunt who lived in a house with a magical garden. It was full of flowers and had a large lawn bordered with a buxus hedge.

Only on special occasions were we allowed to go beyond the hedge to the part of the garden with the pond and the tree with the blue plums, whose heavily laden branches hung over the pond. The plums looked so plump and inviting with the dusty bloom covering their skins, and they had a wonderfully sweet scent. I always regarded this place as a secret garden. Even though you can now buy red, orange and even yellow plums, the blue plums are, to me, by far the nicest.

September plums panel

The finished design measures
21 x 16cm (8½ x 6½in)

YOU WILL NEED

36-count cream linen,
approx. 36 x 31cm (14 x 12½in)
Stranded embroidery thread as
given in the key
No. 24 tapestry needle
Strong board or card
Strong thread for lacing
Mount and frame of your choice

THE EMBROIDERY

1 Cut out the linen, bearing in mind the amount you would like to remain visible between the stitched design and the frame. The amount suggested for this project will result in 7.5cm (3in) of unstitched fabric all around the design.

2 Prepare the linen as outlined on pages 138–140. Find the centre of the fabric, then carefully mark the central vertical and horizontal lines with basting stitches.

3 Find the centre of the cross stitch chart and mark it for your reference. With one

strand of embroidery thread in the needle, begin stitching from this point. Work each cross stitch over two threads of the fabric, ensuring that the upper threads of each stitch go in the same direction.

4 Follow the 'September plums' chart until the the cross stitching is complete,

using the key for the colours of embroidery thread to be used. Each square of the chart represents one stitch.

FINISHING

1 When complete, remove the embroidery from the hoop or frame and hand wash it carefully in warm water. Lay the the piece

of embroidery face down on a towel and press with a hot iron until it is dry.

2 Choose a mount and frame to suit the 'September plums' design. Cut a piece of board or card to fit the frame and mount the embroidery as described on page 141. To finish, set the mount in the frame.

SEPTEMBER PLUMS *key*

	DMC	ANCHOR		DMC	ANCHOR
	319	1044		554	95
	3363	262		3747	120
	3346	267		772	259
	939	152		895	1044
	520	862		522	860
	502	877		3347	266
	989	242		524	858
	211	342		930	1035
	793	176		471	265
	367	216		955	203
	932	1033		987	244
	3042	870		3348	264
	823	152		3024	388
	500	683		986	246
	791	178		3041	871
	794	175		3022	8581
	792	941		503	876
	341	117		562	210
	931	1034		3371	382
	320	215		3787	904
	501	878		561	212
	368	214		3021	905
	369	1043		895	1044
	340	118		3345	268

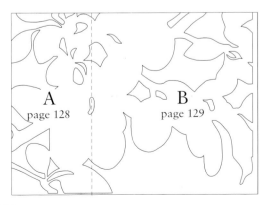

A page 128

B page 129

The chart for the 'September plums' panel has been split over two pages. Refer to this diagram to check the relevant page on which each section of the chart falls.

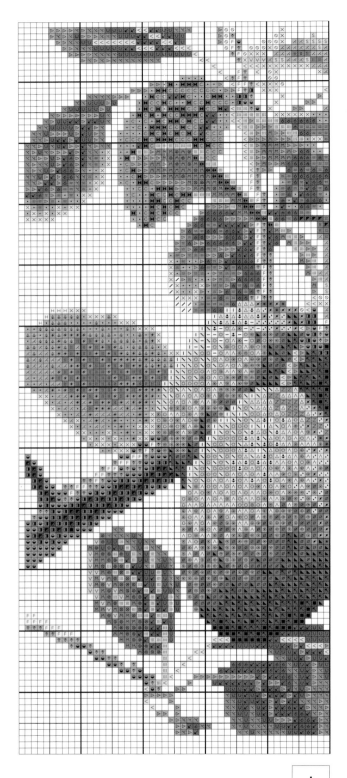

A

B

Bilberries

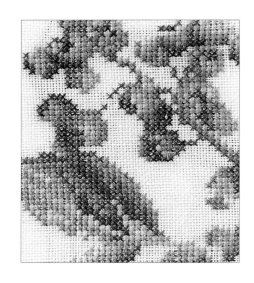

THIS CHARMING cross stitch panel features clusters of small, dark blue bilberries ripening on the branch. These delicately scented little fruit come from the Vaccinium family; the Latin name means 'the colour of a hyacinth'.

If picked when ripe and soft, bilberries can be eaten raw with sugar and cream. However, they can taste sour and I prefer them baked in a pie, lightly stewed with sugar or, better still, in bilberry jam. Jam-making is one of my favourite ways of spending time in the kitchen. I love cooking the fruit and sugar until it is a rich syrupy mixture, and the smell of hot bilberries is quite mouthwatering. I used to make so much jam with my bilberry crop each year that my family called for a temporary suspension on jam-making, to allow them to catch up with supplies!

Bilberries panel

The finished design measures
17 x 12.5cm (6³/₄ x 5in)

YOU WILL NEED

36-count white linen,
approx. 24.5 x 20cm (9¹/₂ x 8in)
Stranded embroidery thread as
given in the key
No. 24 tapestry needle
Mount of your choice
Strong board or card
Strong thread for lacing
Mount and frame of your choice

THE EMBROIDERY

1 Cut out the fabric, bearing in mind the amount you would like to remain visible between the stitched design and the frame. The amount suggested above will result in about 7.5cm (3in) of unstitched fabric all around the design.

2 Prepare the fabric as outlined on pages 138–140. Find the centre of the fabric and carefully mark the central vertical and horizontal lines with basting stitches.

3 Find the centre of the chart and mark it for your reference. With one strand of

Vaccinium augustifolium

embroidery thread in the needle, begin stitching the design from this point. Work each cross stitch over two threads of the fabric, ensuring that all the upper threads of each stitch go in the same direction.

4 Follow the 'Bilberries' panel chart to complete the cross stitching; each square of the chart represents one stitch.

5 Complete the back stitch details using one strand of embroidery thread in the needle, and referring to the key for colours of thread to be used.

FINISHING

1 Remove the finished embroidery from the hoop or frame and hand wash it in warm water. Then lay the 'Bilberries' embroidery face down on a towel and press with a hot iron until it is dry.

2 Choose a mount and frame that will co-ordinate with the colour in the design and with your furnishings. Cut a piece of board or card to fit the frame and mount the embroidery as explained on page 141. Set the mount in the frame.

BILBERRIES PANEL *key*

DMC	ANCHOR		DMC	ANCHOR
3384	264		3012	855
3364	261		3011	856
3347	266		975	357
3346	267		3826	1049
3345	268		844	1041
895	1044		504	206
3753	1031		320	215
3752	1032		367	216
932	1033		319	1044
931	1034		890	218
930	1035		3755	140
3750	1036		322	978
327	101		312	979
503	876		838	1088
502	877		501	878
3013	853		300	352

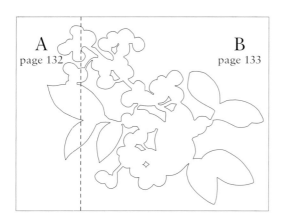

A page 132   B page 133

The chart for the 'Bilberries' panel has been split over two pages. Refer to this diagram to check the relevant page on which each section of the chart falls.

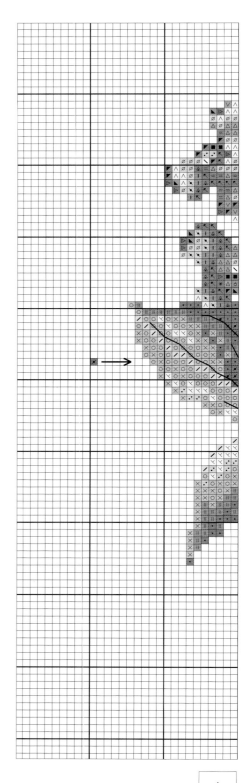

A

B

Apples

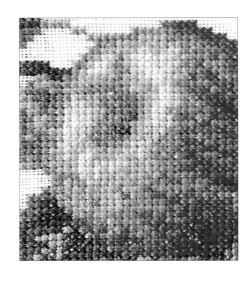

A S WELL as being consumed with relish, the humble apple has been painted, photographed and sculptured time and time again. Increasingly in the last few years, it has also been used as a decoration in flower arrangements.

I like to incorporate apples in my still-life designs, for example when stitching a picture of fresh fruit on a plate or in a basket, or placed next to a vase of flowers. Sun-blushed apples in particular make lovely subjects. Part of the appeal lies in their glorious colours, which cover the spectrum from dark red and pink to yellow and green and almost brown. Apples also have a satisfyingly spherical shape, unpunctuated by bumps, which is perfectly offset by their smooth, shiny skin. These apples look so sweet and tempting, you could almost bite into them.

Apples box

The finished design measures
14 x 9.5cm (5½ x 3¾in)

YOU WILL NEED

28-count white linen,
approx. 21.5 x 17cm (8½ x 6¾in)
Stranded embroidery thread as
given in the key
No. 24 tapestry needle
Mount of your choice
Strong board or card
Strong thread for lacing
Rectangular wooden box
with a panelled frame lid

THE EMBROIDERY

1 Cut the linen to the required size and prepare for stitching, as outlined on pages 138–140. Find the centre of the fabric and carefully mark the central vertical and horizontal lines with basting stitches.

2 Find the centre of the 'Apple box' chart and mark it for your reference. Working with one strand of embroidery thread in the needle, begin stitching the design from this point, working each cross stitch over two threads of the fabric, and ensuring that all the upper threads of the stitch go in the same direction.

3 Follow the chart to complete the cross stitching. Each square represents one stitch.

4 Complete the back stitch details, using one strand of thread and referring to the key for colours of thread to be used.

FINISHING

1 Remove the finished embroidery from the hoop or frame and hand wash it in warm water. When the embroidery is nearly dry, lay face down on a towel and press with a hot iron.

2 You could use any type of box you prefer to display this project. I had the box pictured above made up specially by a framer, and thought that it would make an attractive gift. Cut a piece of board or card to fit the lid of the box and mount the 'Apples' embroidery, as described on page 141. Set the mount in the panel of the box to finish.

Alternatively, you could simply frame the embroidery and hang it on the wall. Choose a mount and frame to co-ordinate with the colours in the design. Cut a piece of board or card to fit the frame and mount the embroidery as described on page 141. Set the mount in the frame.

APPLE BOX *key*

	DMC	ANCHOR		DMC	ANCHOR		DMC	ANCHOR
○ ○	632	936	∨ ∨	3053	843	▼ ▼	676	891
× ×	368	214	■ ■	3021	905	◤ ◤	402	1047
‖ ‖	3345	268	⋋ ⋋	3022	8581	◔ ◔	725	305
· ·	989	242	6 6	734	279	◤ ◤	3777	1015
◤ ◤	3346	267	I I	352	9	▣ ▣	817	13
\ \	746	275	▲ ▲	3052	844	T T	922	1003
ø ø	3347	266	▷ ▷	351	10	♡ ♡	729	890
∧ ∧	839	1086	◥ ◥	677	361	⅄ ⅄	470	266
◤ ◤	895	1044	✳ ✳	471	265	Y Y	745	300
◤ ◤	838	1088	⦀ ⦀	642	392	✚ ✚	3013	853
↖ ↖	3051	845	H H	3348	264	⊡ ⊡	3830	5975
∴ ∴	3772	1007	M M	936	846	⊡ ⊡	722	323
= =	350	11	< <	472	253	4 4	367	216
⊙ ⊙	3787	904	⊗ ⊗	935	861	⊖ ⊖	937	268
- -	772	259	Z Z	644	391	⬥ ⬥	726	295

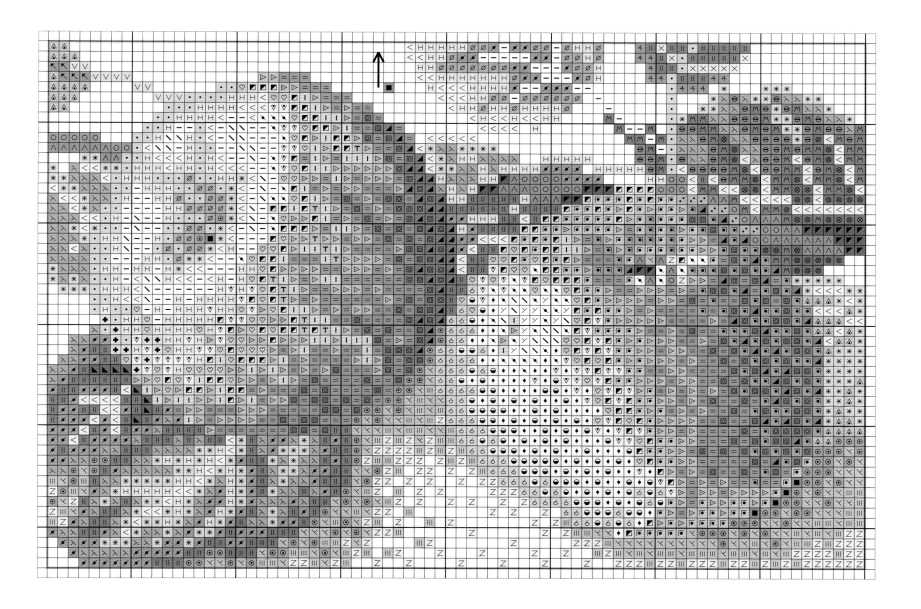

Materials and Techniques

CROSS STITCH does not involve a huge outlay of materials. All you need to get started are a few basics, which are detailed below. Fabrics, embroidery threads, needles and frames are all easily available from needlework shops.

The basic stitches used in cross stitch are explained here, illustrated with diagrams, together with advice on stitching with beads and blending threads. There are also guidelines on how to finish the work, by mounting pictures, making up cushions and edging table linen.

Materials

Yarns

DMC embroidery threads are used throughout, as the choice of colours is excellent, although there are other brands of thread you can use. Anchor alternatives have been listed, but the colours may not match the DMC colours exactly. The instructions for each project specify the number of strands of thread to use. One strand of thread is used for both cross stitch and back stitch for all the designs; however, it is possible to use two threads to strengthen the impact of a design, such as the petals on the 'Pear blossom' design. One skein of each colour is usually sufficient for each project, but if more skeins are required, this is stated in the key.

Cut the embroidery thread into 50cm (20in) lengths to aid your stitching; longer lengths will easily become tangled and knotted, and ruin your work.

Needles

Always use a tapestry needle for cross stitch work as the end is rounded and blunt which prevents it piercing the fibres of the fabric, and your fingers. Tapestry needles are available in different sizes. For most cross stitch work, a medium size No. 24 needle is comfortable to use, but you may prefer a thinner or larger needle. Experiment to find the best for you.

Fabrics

Linen is often used for cross stitch as it gives a very fine finish. This is a natural fabric so the thickness of the threads can vary across the fabric. Cross stitches are usually stitched over two threads of the fabric. As linen is a natural fabric, the finished stitching will have an irregular, uneven look, which many stitchers prefer. Aida fabric is also used for cross stitch. It has a surface of clearly designated squares and, as each stitch covers one square, it is easier to count the stitches. Stitching on Aida produces a more even finish than stitching on linen.

Aida and linen are both available in a variety of colours and it is fun replacing the usual white, cream or beige fabric with an unusual colour, such as black, navy or even pink. A coloured fabric can completely change the effect of a design, either complementing it or throwing it into sharp relief (see above).

It is important to know the 'count' of the piece of fabric you are using, as this will determine the finished size of your

stitching. All fabrics have a count, which for Aida fabric refers to the number of blocks and therefore stitches per inch; the higher the count, the smaller the finished stitching. Popular Aida counts are 14- and 18-count; the latter fabric produces the finest stitching and the smallest finished design. The linen count refers to the number of threads per inch. As linen is worked over two threads per stitch, the thread count should be halved to find out the stitch count per inch. For example, 28-count linen, which has 28 threads per inch, gives a stitch count of 14.

When considering how many strands of thread to use with different counts of fabric, I use the following as a guide. When stitching on linen with 26 threads per inch or Aida with 12 blocks per inch, you should use two strands of thread. When stitching on linen with 30 or 32 threads per inch, or on Aida with 14 or 16 blocks per inch, you should use one strand of embroidery thread.

Altering the count of fabric used for your stitching gives you the flexibility to alter the overall effects of your embroidery, enabling you to make a design larger or smaller, bolder or more delicate.

Techniques

Preparation

Before you actually begin stitching, some preparation will be required. Although it takes a bit of time, it will actually save time later, and helps to produce a more professional finish to your stitching.

Fabric

Each project contains a complete list of the materials you will require. The measurements given for the fabric include at least 7cm (2³/4in) all around to allow for preparing the edges and for stretching the fabric in a frame. Many evenweave fabrics tend to fray easily, especially when being handled. Before you begin stitching, therefore, it is advisable either to oversew the edges of the fabric with ordinary sewing thread, or to stick masking tape around the edges to prevent fraying.

Find the centre of the fabric, as this is the best place to start stitching. Fold the fabric in half both ways, creasing along the fold lines. Open the fabric out and stitch long basting stitches along both the horizontal and vertical crease lines, running from edge to edge of the fabric. Where the lines cross is the centre point. The basting stitches can be removed later.

Using a hoop

It is advisable to use an embroidery hoop or frame when stitching as it keeps the fabric taut and does not let it stretch or distort, making stitching easier. For small pieces of embroidery, a hoop is the most popular frame. It consists of two rings, one fitted inside the other. To stretch the piece of fabric in a hoop, place the area to be stitched over the inner ring, then press the outer ring over the fabric, with the tension screw released. When the fabric is taut and the weave is straight (check the basted horizontal and vertical lines), tighten the tension screw. If the fabric creases, release the outer ring and repeat. Embroidery hoops are available in several different sizes, ranging from 10cm (4in) to 38cm (15in) in diameter. Hoops with table stands or floor stands attached are also available.

Using a frame

If working on some of the larger pieces of embroidery, rectangular slate frames are also available. They consist of two rollers, with tapes attached, and two flat side pieces, which slot into the rollers and are held in place by pegs or screws. Slate frames are available in sizes ranging from 30cm (12in) to 68cm (27in). To stretch your fabric in a rectangular frame, baste a

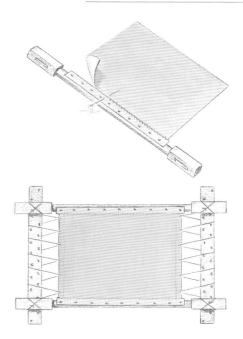

12mm (¹/2in) turning on the top and the bottom edges of the fabric, and oversew strong tape to the other two sides (in addition to the masking tape used earlier).

Working from the centre outwards, oversew the top and bottom edges to the roller tapes with strong thread. Fit the side pieces into the slots, and roll any extra fabric on one roller until the fabric is completely taut. Insert the pegs or screws to secure the frame. Lace both edges of the fabric using a large-eyed needle threaded with strong thread; secure the ends around the intersections of the frame. Lace the webbing at 2.5cm (1in) intervals, stretching the fabric evenly.

Threads

Once you have prepared the fabric, then you need to organize your embroidery threads. Cut a supply of 50cm (20in) lengths of the threads you will need for the project, separating them into the required number of strands, and threading them in a thread organizer. This is a piece of card with holes punched down each side. Each colour can be threaded and looped through a different hole, and labelled with the correct colour number. When you need to use a particular thread, simply unloop a length from the organizer, and thread it in your needle.

Stitching

Cross stitch is very simple to do. Always start at the centre of the fabric and work outwards, as this ensures that the design will be placed centrally on the fabric. The centre is where the basted horizontal and vertical lines cross. Find the centre of the chart before you start stitching and mark it for your reference.

Never start or finish with a knot in the embroidery thread, as this will look unsightly when the piece is finished. When you begin, leave a long thread end at the back of the fabric, holding it with a finger initially, then catch the thread with the first few stitches to hold it secure. Check on the back of your work that this thread has been secured before letting it go. When finishing stitching, either to change colour or because the thread has run out, weave the thread end through the back of four or five nearby stitches, then trim.

If stitching an area that features several tiny areas of colour close together, you might find it helpful to work with a few needles at once. This saves you continually finishing one colour and starting another, and creating lumps of thread ends at the back, all of which involves the repeated threading of one needle. If you are using several needles at once, take care to keep them pinned to the fabric at one side of the work or you may lose track of them. Also, be careful not to stitch over and

trap the loose threads at the back caused by using several colours at one time.

Cross stitch

To make one cross stitch, think of the stitch area as a square. Bring the needle up through the hole in the bottom right of the square then take it down through the hole in the top left of the square. Then take the needle up through the bottom left hole and down into the top right.

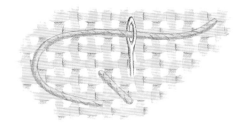

In order to stitch a row of cross stitches, work from right to left, completing the first row of evenly spaced diagonal stitches over the number of threads of the fabric specified in the project instructions.

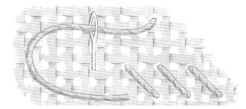

Then, working from left to right, repeat the process to finish the stitches. Always make sure that each cross stitch crosses in the same direction.

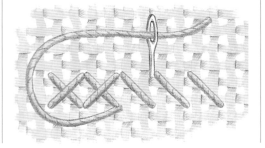

Back stitch

This stitch is used to outline part of a design, or to indicate a foldline or shadow. Back stitch is indicated on the chart by a bold line; the colour of the back stitch is denoted by a symbol which is arrowed to the line. The chart key lists each symbol next to its colour of thread; some of the back stitch symbols are the same as the cross stitch symbols.

Each back stitch is worked over the same number of threads as the cross stitch to form a continuous line. Bring the needle up from behind the work and down through the fabric one stitch length behind the first point. Pass the needle under the fabric, and then up one stitch length ahead of the first point. Repeat and continue in this way.

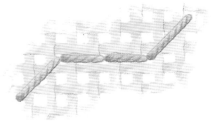

Embellishing a design

Blending threads

A pleasing effect can be achieved by incorporating blending filament. This is a fine sparkly thread that can be used with stranded cotton to add shine and texture, and works to highlight areas of a design. However, blending filament does not move through the fabric as easily as stranded cotton and care needs to be taken when stitching with it. Use the blending filament in short lengths in order to prevent the thread tangling and to stop the fibres 'stripping' off as the thread is pulled through the fabric.

Dampen the blending filament before using it. To thread blending filament, double the thread about 5cm (2in) at one end, and insert the loop through the eye of the needle. Pull the loop over the point of the needle and gently pull the loop towards the end of the eye to secure the thread to the needle. If you are using a combination of blending filament and stranded cotton, thread the latter through the eye in the usual way, and trim it to match the length of the blending filament.

Beading

Some designs can be embellished by the use of beads, which are available in a wide variety of colours, sheens and sizes. For example, you could stitch beads in the centre of cross stitch flowers for added depth and sparkle. Using beads adds extra texture to a cross stitch design, and works especially well on dark colours. Add beads to a design after the stitching is complete, in order to prevent the beads breaking in the embroidery hoop. Begin the stitch by bringing a beading needle up at the bottom left of the square, then thread the needle through a bead before bringing the needle down through the top right of the square in order to complete

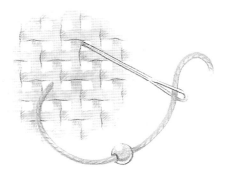

the half cross stitch. The diagonal stitch should follow the direction of the second half of a cross stitch.

Using charts

Each project in the book has a chart detailing what colours to stitch where; each square of the chart represents one stitch. Some of the charts are, due to space constrictions, smaller than is practicable. Likewise, some of the charts, because of their size, are spread over several pages. For ease of working, you will find that it is easier to photocopy, and enlarge, the chart before beginning to stitch. Then you can tape together the sections of chart for a more coherent overall stitch plan.

Always start from the centre of the chart and work outwards. Some stitchers like to tick off the squares or colour them in as they stitch to make it easier to follow the chart. Alternatively, you might prefer to use a ruler to aid your stitching, and move it down line by line as needed.

Finishing

After you have finished stitching, remove the hoop and trim any straggly thread ends on the back of the fabric. If the completed embroidery is a bit dirty, you can wash it carefully in hand hot water. Use a gentle cleanser but not a detergent and agitate gently, rather than scrubbing.

Rinse, then place the embroidery face down on a towel. When nearly dry, press it lightly with a warm iron on the reverse side to smooth out any creases. Using a towel prevents the threads being flattened by the iron. Then mount the embroidery for framing, sew it to a piece of backing fabric to make a cushion, or create a decorative edge for table linen.

Mounting embroidery

A professional framer will mount and frame a piece of embroidery, but if you would prefer to do this yourself, here is the basic method.

Cut a piece of plywood to the size of the finished embroidery, with an extra amount added all round to allow for the recess in the frame. Mark both the central vertical and horizontal lines on the piece of plywood. Place the embroidery face down and centre the plywood on top so that the basted lines on the fabric and the drawn lines on the plywood match.

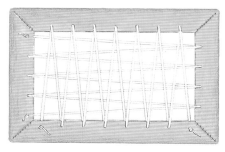

Fold over the edges of the fabric on opposite sides, making mitred folds at the corners, and lace across, using strong thread. Repeat on the other two sides. Finally, pull up the stitches tightly to stretch the fabric firmly. Then overstitch the mitred corners to neaten. Check that the design is still centred on the front.

An alternative method to lacing the fabric is to staple the fabric to the piece of plywood after first mitring the corners as before. The mounted embroidery should now be ready for framing.

Making a cushion cover

The finished embroidery can be used as the front panel of the cushion cover, or you can stitch it on to a front piece. Either way, you then need to cut out two pieces of backing fabric for the back of the cover. These should be the same width as the front panel, and each slightly more than half the length of the front panel. When these are placed on top of the front cover panel, they should overlap in the centre. Turn and stitch the central overlapping sides of each back panel, one with a larger turning than the other.

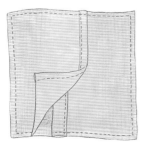

Place the front embroidered panel flat, with the embroidery facing upwards. Then place the two prepared pieces of backing fabric on top, with the raw edges matching and hemmed edges overlapping in the centre and facing upwards. Ensure that the larger central hem lies beneath the smaller one. Pin, then stitch around all four sides, taking a 1.5cm (1/2in) seam. Remove the pins, then turn the right side out through the central flap and press.

Envelope-flap cushion covers can be left as they are, but adding buttons to the back flap gives them a decorative finish. Mark the position of three buttons on the right side of the central flap, using tailor's chalk. Using a sewing machine threaded with matching thread, stitch the button-holes on the top flap; these consist of two rows of parallel zigzag stitches. The length of the buttonhole opening should equal the diameter of the button plus its height. Place pins at each end of the buttonhole to prevent cutting through the end stitches. Using a seam ripper, slit the fabric down the centre of the buttonhole stitches.

Sew the three buttons in position on the lower flap. Insert a cushion pad and fasten the buttons to complete.

Edging table linen

There are several ways of edging table linen. The simplest method is to turn under the hem edges twice and stitch the hem by hand or by machine on all four sides. For a neater effect, you can mitre the corners of the piece before hemming. To do this, press a single hem to the wrong side. Then open the hem out again

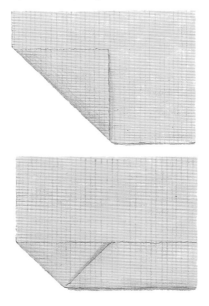

and fold the corner of the fabric inwards. Refold the hem to the wrong side along the pressed line, and slip stitch in place.

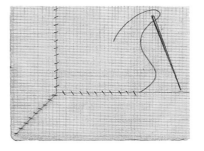

For a more decorative finish, you could fringe the edging around all four sides. To do this, trim the fabric to the required size, then simply pull four threads away on all sides. To prevent the fringe fraying further, stitch a line of straight stitches in place two threads (for linen), or one square (for Aida), inside the frayed edge.

An alternative method of edging is hem stitching, which gives an ornamental finish to table linen. Trim the fabric to the required size plus turnings. Then measure a double hem width in from the raw edges and remove the next six threads on each of the four sides. This forms the hem line.

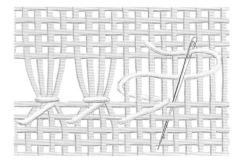

Using one strand of embroidery thread, in the same colour as the fabric, hem stitch around the edges of the fabric as follows. Working on the wrong side and from right to left, bring the needle up two threads inside the hem line. Then take the needle across three threads and insert it to pass beneath these threads from right to left. Bring the needle out again, pass it in front of the looped threads and insert it behind the fabric to emerge two threads down ready to make the next stitch. Before inserting the needle, pull the threads tight, so that the bound threads form a neat group.

Repeat all around the fabric, then hem stitch on the outer side of the drawn threads around the fabric. To finish, hem or fringe the fabric edges all around, mitring corners if desired.

AUTHOR'S ACKNOWLEDGMENTS

Thank you to everyone who has made it possible for me to work on this book – in particular to Jeremy Hamilton, Karen Hemingway, Heather Dewhurst and Rowena Curtis. A special thanks must also go to the stitching ladies who made up all the cross stitch designs so beautifully.

ACKNOWLEDGMENTS

The publishers wish to acknowledge the assistance of the following:

Mark Sugden
Frames by Design
20 Burners Lane
Kiln Farm
Milton Keynes
MK11 3HB
tel: + 44 1908 262 681
For framing the embroidered panels for photography.

Permin of Copenhagen Linens
Enquiries: please contact
Michael Whitaker Fabrics (see above right for details)
For supplying the backing linen for the Tulip display cushion, pages 12–17.

Rose & Hubble Ltd
2/4 Relay Road
London
W12 7SJ
tel: + 44 208 749 8822

For supplying the cotton inset for the Rose and ribbons cushion, pages 64–7.

S & A Frames
The Old Post Office
Yarra Road
Cleethorpes
North Lincolnshire
DN35 8LS
tel: + 44 1472 697 772
For supplying the Apple box frame, pages 134–7.

GENERAL SUPPLIERS

For information on your nearest stockist of stranded cotton, contact the following:

DMC
UK
DMC Creative World Ltd
62 Pullman Road
Wigston
Leicester
LE8 2DY
tel: + 44 1162 811 040

USA
The DMC Corporation
Port Kearny Building
10 South Kearny
NJ 07032
tel: + 1 973 344 0299

AUSTRALIA
DMC Needlecraft Pty Ltd
PO Box 317
Earlwood
NSW 2206
tel: + 61 2 9559 3088

COATS AND ANCHOR
UK
Coats Crafts UK
PO Box 22
McMullen Road
Darlington
Co. Durham
DL1 1YQ
tel: + 44 1325 394 394

USA
Coats North America
4135 South Stream Blvd
Charlotte
North Carolina 28217
tel: + 1 704 329 5800

AUSTRALIA
Coats Paton Crafts
Level 1
382 Wellington Road
Mulgrave
Victoria 3170
tel: + 61 3 9561 2288

KIT SUPPLIERS

Fa. Thea Gouverneur bv
Hoofdstraat 78a
2171 AV Sassenheim
The Netherlands
tel: + 31 252 214 453
fax: + 31 252 224 067

Michael Whitaker Fabrics
15/16 Midland Mills
Station Road
Crosshills
Keighley
West Yorkshire BD20 7DT
UK
tel: + 44 1535 636 903

Interline Imports Inc
1050880 Ainsworth Crescent
Richmond BC 7A 3V6
Canada
tel: + 1 604 271 8242

Potpourri Etc.
275 Church Street
Chillicote Street Oh 45601
USA
tel: + 1 740 779 9512

Joan Togitt/Zweigart
262 Old New Brunswick Road
Piscataway NJ 08854
USA
tel: + 1 732 562 8888

Ristal Threads
Heritage Village
Unit 11/12
2602 Watson Act
Australia
tel: + 61 2 62 412 293

Penguin Threads Pty Ltd
25–27 Izett Street
Prahran
Victoria 3181
Australia
tel: + 61 395 294 400

Yuki Ltd
10-10-4-Bancho Karakuen
Nishinomiya City
622-0088 Japan
tel: + 81 798 721 563
(Also suppliers of Anchor stranded cotton.)

Index